COEDICION LATINOAMERICA

ENCUENTRAME

FIESTAS POPULARES DE AMERICA LATINA

Quinta impresión, 1998

Colaboraron con el presente volumen: Editorial Gente Nueva, *Cuba*
Editorial Andrés Bello, *Chile* • Ministerio de Educación y Cultura, *Ecuador*
Editorial Nueva Nicaragua, *Nicaragua* • Credisol Publicaciones, *Uruguay*
ISBN 980-257-059-1 • Impreso en Caracas por Intenso Offset,1998

Coordinacion: Ediciones Ekare - Banco del Libro • Editora: Veronica Uribe • Diseño: Irene Savino

Mi nombre es Chico y vivo
en San Luis de Paraitinga.
En esta semana, en mi ciudad,
estamos celebrando la fiesta
del **Divino Espíritu Santo.**
Va a haber misa, procesión, bailes,
cantos, cohetes, comida para todo
el mundo y mucha diversión
con los muñecos Juan Paulino
y María Angú.
¡ENCUENTRAME!

Ilustración: Ricardo Azevedo

Me llamo Pedro y vivo en Pomaire, un pueblo campesino donde hacemos cerámicas que son famosas en todo el país.
Hoy estamos celebrando el **18 de Septiembre,** el aniversario de nuestra Independencia.
Hay juegos y competencias, cantos y bailes, empanadas y pan amasado... y mucha alegría.
Yo estoy en medio de la fiesta.
¡ENCUENTRAME!

Ilustración: Francisco Olivares Thomsen

COLOMBIA

Mi nombre es Manuela y vivo en Riosucio. Estamos celebrando el **Carnaval del Diablo.** En este momento se inicia un desfile que conduce a su majestad el diablo a la plaza. Lo acompañan un cortejo de enmascarados, un grupo de músicos, y al fondo, una comparsa Los riosuceños nos divertimos disfrazándonos, cantando, quemando pólvora y bailando... ¡ENCUENTRAME!

Ilustración: Alekos

CUBA

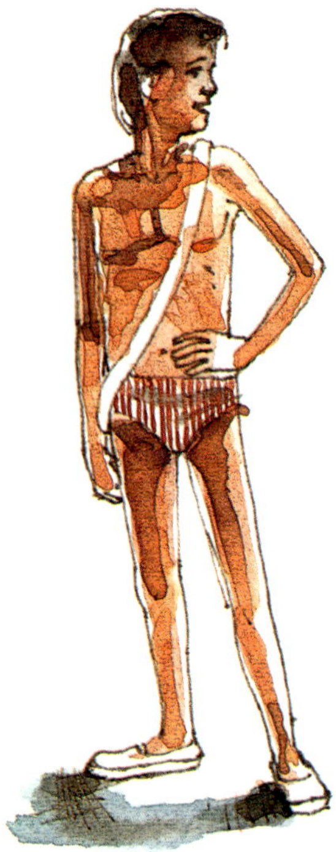

Yo soy Pedrito, un cubanito
que vive en Cojimar,
al lado mismo del mar.
Y como hoy es domingo,
estoy pasando un buen rato
en el **Plan de la Calle**
de mi cuadra. Algunos
de los muchachos del barrio
compiten en las carreras con sacos,
unos disfrutan de la playa,
otros bailan o saltan a la suiza,
y yo... pues...
¡ENCUENTRAME!

ESTAURANTE
LA TERRAZA
Plan de LA CaLLE

ECUADOR

Me llamo Andrés.
Vivo en Cuenca, en el barrio de San Sebastián.
Es Navidad y, al igual que toda la población, estoy participando en el **Pase del Niño**:
¡ENCUENTRAME!

Ilustración: Mariana Kuonqui

NICARAGUA

Soy Jimmy Colomer y vivo allí,
en Old Bank, un barrio
de la ciudad de Bluefields.
Estamos celebrando **Mayo-ya**
y todos bailamos con cintas
alrededor del palo.
Cantamos, comemos guabul
y rondón y la gente mayor
bebe mucho ron.
La fiesta de **Mayo-ya** me gusta
mucho.
¡ENCUENTRAME!

Ilustración: Ernesto Chamorro López (Tito)

PERU

Me llamo Jacinta y vivo en la sierra,
en el pueblo de Ondores.
Estamos en el último día
de carnavales, celebrando la **yunsa**
o **cortamonte.**
La gente está muy alegre.
Unos bailan y tiran serpentinas,
otros comen y unos pocos nos
divertimos jugando con agua, talco
y papel picado...
¡ENCUENTRAME!

Ilustración: Gredna Landolt Pardo

PUERTO RICO

Mi nombre es Teresa y vivo
en Loíza Aldea, muy cerca
de la playa.
En estos días nuestro poblado
está celebrando las fiestas
de **Santiago Apóstol.**
Hoy estuve en la procesión
con mis amigos y ahora estoy aquí
tratando de esconderme
para que los vejigantes
no me hagan maldades.
¡ENCUENTRAME!

Ilustración: Yolanda Pastrana Fuentes

URUGUAY

Somos Martín y Carolina, dos niños
uruguayos del campo.
Gervasio, nuestro padre,
es domador y en Semana Santa
va a competir en las domas
de **la Criolla** que se organizan
en un pueblo cercano.
Nuestra madre, que es muy buena
cocinera, hace pasteles y tortas
fritas para vender.
Todos disfrutan de la fiesta...
¡ENCUENTRANOS!

Ilustración: Washington Algaré

VENEZUELA

Me llamo Iginia y vivo en Chuao,
un pueblo que queda al lado
del mar.
Hoy es el día de **San Juan**
y tenemos procesión y baile
de tambor.
Todo el mundo está en la calle
viendo cómo pasean al santo.
Los tambores están empezando
a sonar...
¡ENCUENTRAME!

Ilustración: Laura Liberatore

BRASIL

La fiesta del **Divino Espíritu Santo** se celebra todos los años en la última semana del mes de mayo, en el pueblo de San Luis de Paraitinga, en el interior del estado de Sao Paulo.
Es una fiesta de sello religioso, mezclada con antiguas tradiciones populares. Se celebra después de la cosecha, por lo tanto, es una fiesta de alegría, agradecimiento y pago de promesas. Una procesión va de casa en casa cantando y pidiendo donativos y prendas. Durante los festejos, además de las misas, procesiones, bailes y cantos, hay comida gratis para todos.
De vez en cuando, aparecen unos muñecos, Juan Paulino, María Angú y el Buey que corren tras los niños, inventando juegos y haciendo travesuras.

CHILE

La celebración del **18 de Septiembre** se remonta a los primeros años de vida independiente.
Los historiadores recuerdan que en estos días de fiesta, la gente se reunía en lugares al aire libre, levantaban *ramadas,* preparaban comidas típicas, bebían vino y chicha, bailaban y cantaban acompañados de arpa, guitarra, tamborines y triángulos.
Niños y adultos participaban en los más diversos juegos y competencias: carreras de ensacados, el palo ensebado, carreras de caballos, riñas de gallos y competencias de volantines.
Hoy día, la celebración es similar en todos los pueblos campesinos.
Pomaire se encuentra en la zona central de Chile, a unos 50 kilómetros de Santiago. Es famoso por las tradicionales cerámicas que se fabrican allí desde antes de la llegada de los españoles.

---

ramadas: cobertizos o toldos hechos con ramas de árboles

COLOMBIA

s habitantes de Riosucio, al ccidente de Colombia, celebran da dos años el **Carnaval del iablo.** Este personaje, que se presenta por medio de una estatua cuatro metros, hecha en fibra de drio, vigila todas las ceremonias. carnaval es ante todo una fiesta blada, famosa por los saludos que hacen al diablo y por el ingenio de s canciones que aluden a oblemas nacionales, del pueblo, o situaciones cotidianas. El último a, los riosuceños se disfrazan de udas y plañideras y entre lamentos ánticos queman un diablo de apo y le dan sepultura.

CUBA

Los domingos o días festivos, se organizan los **planes de la calle** para disfrute de los *fiñes*.
Se cierra la cuadra con sogas, barriles o latones y en ese espacio se hacen competencias de carreras con sacos, patines, bicicletas; se juega al chucho escondido, a los agarrados, se salta a la suiza, se baila, en fin, se disfruta de nuestro sol y de la alegría de vivir.
Se premia a los ganadores con libros, libretas, lápices, juguetes y se merienda bocaditos, dulces, caramelos, refrescos, helados.

---

fiñes: muchachos

ECUADOR

Año tras año, entre el primer domingo de adviento y el martes de carnaval se celebra en Cuenca el **Pase del Niño.** En esta fiesta, los niños hacen la corte a una imagen del niño Dios y danzan al compás de tonos que combinan la alegría y la tristeza del acontecimiento de Belén. La fiesta llega a su máximo esplendor en la mañana del 24 de diciembre con el Pase del Niño Viajero cuando cuadras y cuadras de la ciudad se llenan de gente, colorido y música para celebrar el nacimiento del Niño Jesús.

(Tomado del prólogo de Claudio Malo a la obra **El Pase del Niño,** *de Susana González, Universidad de Cuenca, 1981, p.14).*

NICARAGUA

Bluefields es una región de Nicaragua situada en la Costa Atlántica que hasta finales del siglo pasado fue colonia de Inglaterra. Por ese motivo, han perdurado allí los nombres ingleses y manifestaciones culturales muy particulares.
La mayor parte de los habitantes son descendientes de esclavos africanos, pero también viven en esta región indios miskitos, sumos y ramas.
Con **Mayo-ya** celebramos la fertilidad en espera de las primeras lluvias. A esta fiesta se le llama también **Palo de Mayo** porque el baile principal consiste en ir cruzando cintas de colores que cuelgan de un árbol para luego, al ritmo del baile, volver a dejarlas en orden.
Después, la gente recorre las calles de la ciudad de Bluefields, cantando y bailando al son de pitos, clarinetes, violines y tambores.
También se juega el *palo lucio,* y se come *guabul* y *rondón.*

Fernando Silva

---

palo lucio: palo ensebado
guabul y rondón: comidas típicas hechas con banano, leche, coco, carne y pescado.

PERU

En los pueblos del valle del Mantaro, en los Andes Peruanos, así como en otros lugares de la sierra y costa del país, es tradicional la celebración de la fiesta de la **yunsa,** conocida también como **cortamonte** o **tumbamonte.**
La **yunsa** es parte central de la festividad de los carnavales y en ocasiones también se celebra para festejar el cambio de estación.
Para celebrarla, los organizadores plantan previamente un árbol de tronco grueso y muy ramoso. En sus ramas cuelgan dulces, juguetes, globos y objetos artesanales.
Desde muy temprano, las parejas forman un círculo y bailan en torno al árbol. Al son de las guitarras, arpa, violín y *tinya,* van turnándose un hacha con la que golpean el tronco hasta que lo derriban.
Cuando el árbol cae, todos gritan entusiasmados y se precipitan a coger los objetos. La pareja que asestó el último golpe recibe una canasta con golosinas y potajes que distribuye entre los asistentes y queda con el compromiso de organizar una nueva **yunsa** al año siguiente.

---

tinya: tamborcillo.

PUERTO RICO

Las fiestas de **Santiago Apóstol** empiezan el 25 de julio y cubren toda una semana de jubilosa celebración. Los vecinos se vuelcan sobre las calles para participar de las procesiones y los demás actos religiosos en honor a Santiago de los Muchachos, Santiago de los Hombres y Santiago de las Mujeres.
Luego comienza la fiesta con desfile de *vejigantes* o diablitos, baile de *bomba,* cohetes y fuegos artificiales, competencias deportivas y el disfrute de las *alcapurrias de jueyes* y otros platillos típicos.
La influencia africana es muy evidente en estas fiestas, especialmente en las máscaras, la música y el baile al ritmo de la *bomba* y el *bongó.* Lo que no es de extrañar, pues en otros tiempos toda esa zona costera estuvo habitada por esclavos, que fueron traídos de Africa para trabajar en las plantaciones de caña.
(Fuente consultada: **La fiesta de Santiago Apóstol**, *de Ricardo Alegría).*

Alcapurria de jueyes: empanadilla de cangrejo.
bomba: tambor de madera alto y estrecho, cubierto con cuero de cabra.
bongó: pareja de pequeños tambores hechos con madera y cubiertos de cuero de cabra.
vejigantes: máscaras con aspecto grotesco que representan el mal.

URUGUAY

Al empezar el otoño, en Uruguay el clima se dulcifica, los árboles se cubren de hojas amarillas y un sol suave alienta con la brisa. Llega la Semana Santa, a la que también se llama Semana Criolla o semana de turismo.
En todo el país se organizan fiestas criollas, en homenaje al gaucho, el trabajador del campo cuya existencia se remonta a la época de la independencia.
En **la Criolla** se reviven las tareas más rudas del campo, también diversiones y comidas típicas.
Dentro de un gran ruedo alambrado, los gauchos jinetean potros crudos, ya sea en pelo o ensillados; a veces también se jinetean novillos y se hacen demostraciones de lazo.
Fuera del ruedo, donde está el público, hay *payadores,* es decir, cantores que improvisan sus coplas, a veces en contrapunto con otro, al compás de la guitarra. También se baila, se venden tortas fritas, empanadas y pasteles de dulce.
Hacia otro extremo del predio, en grandes parrillas se asan corderos, vaquillonas con cuero, chorizos y *achuras.*
Mientras esperan, los gauchos toman mate en sus pequeñas calabazas.

---

payadores: cantantes populares que improvisan coplas acompañados de la guitarra.
achuras: intestinos o menudos de la res.

VENEZUELA

La fiesta de **San Juan** se celebra el 24 de junio, desde los tiempos de la Colonia, y es especialmente importante en las zonas donde hubo grandes haciendas de cacao y café, trabajadas por esclavos africanos. El santo se saca de la iglesia en procesión y se le canta y reza a la imagen. En los pueblos costeros, el santo es embarcado y paseado por el mar. Al volver a tierra, comienza el toque de tambores y el baile. Se utilizan diversos tipos de tambores. En la ilustración aparece el mina, un tambor largo que se toca golpeando el cuero y también la madera de los costados.
El tambor más pequeño se llama curbeta. Uno de los bailes preferidos de la fiesta de **San Juan** es el llamado "la perra", en que la mujer trata de tumbar al hombre con golpes de cadera y zancadillas. Cuando logra tumbarlo, otro bailarín sale al ruedo.
(Tomado de: **Fiestas y danzas folklóricas de Venezuela** *de Luis Arturo Domínguez y Adolfo Salazar Quijada. Caracas: Monteávila Editores. 1969).*

Ni
Indian n
cookbook

Indian Vegetarian Cookbook is a complete cookery collection, designed to give confidence and inspiration to not only housewives but all those cooks who like to experiment, whether they are creating a meal for the family or for friends.

With the **Indian Vegetarian Cookbook** besides you, get on with the job of simple yet exotic meals with effortless precision.

Every recipe has been tried to perfection. For any queries about the recipes

E-mail: *nitamehta@nitamehta.com*.
Website: http://www.nitamehta.com

Indian Vegetarian cookbook

Nita Mehta

B.Sc. (Home Science), M.Sc. (Food & Nutrition)
Gold Medalist

SNAB
Publishers Pvt Ltd

Nita Mehta's
Indian Vegetarian
Cookbook

First Paperback Edition 1999, 2nd print 1999

Second Paperback Edition 2000, 1st print 2000, 1st Reprint 2001

ISBN 81-86004-91-2

Food Styling & Photography: SNAB

Layout and laser typesetting:

N.I.T.A. ☎ 3252948
National Information Technology Academy
3A/3, Asaf Ali Road
New Delhi-110002

Published by:

SNAB
Publishers Pvt Ltd
3A/3 Asaf Ali Road
New Delhi-110002

Tel: 91-11-**3250091,** 6214011, **3252948,** 6238727
Fax: 91-11-6235218
E-Mail: snab@snabindia.com;
Website: http://www.snabindia.com
The Best of Cookery Books http://www.nitamehta.com

Printed at:
THOMSON PRESS (INDIA) LIMITED

Distributed by:
THE VARIETY BOOK DEPOT
A.V.G. Bhavan, M 3 Con Circus
New Delhi - 110 001
Tel: 3327175, 3322567; Fax: 3714335

Price: Rs.189/-

PREFACE

Creative cooks – whether housewives or professionals – are always hungry for new ways to practice and improve skills.

Indian Vegetarian Cookbook is a complete cookery collection, designed to give confidence and inspiration to not only housewives but all those cooks who like to experiment, whether they are creating a meal for the family or for friends.

Every recipe in this book has been tried and tested to perfection. The names of the recipes may sound exotic and alarming, but the process has been made much simpler than you expect.

The recipes are made from easily available day-to-day ingredients – none of the high-sounding exported stuff (however, with the Indian market opening up most imported and rare ingredients are also available) – and the method of preparation described in easy-to-follow, step-by-step approach. This time-tested approach has already met with your approval, my dear readers, from over a score of "handy-sized" cookbooks that have received overwhelming response from all of you.

From your tremendous response, feedback and suggestions, here is a cookery reference-cum-workbook on Indian Vegetarian Cookery. This will not only supplement all that you pick up from my smaller cookbooks but it will prove to be an all-time-reference and a single source for "anytime meal" both for the busy housewife and the professional.

With the **Indian Vegetarian Cookbook** besides you, get on with the job of simple yet exotic meals with effortless precision.

Nita Mehta

Contents

How to Prepare Paneer

Paneer is readily available in the market, but due to shortage of milk in summers, paneer becomes scarce in certain parts of India.

To make home made paneer, it is important to use good quality milk. Paneer prepared from full cream milk is certainly softer and tastier than that made from skimmed or toned milk.

To make paneer at home, take out juice of one lemon in a small bowl, carefully removing the seeds. The seeds taste bitter if they come in the paneer by mistake. If there is no lemon, keep one cup of curd ready.

Boil one kilo of full cream milk, stirring continuously to prevent skin forming at the top. When it comes to boil, put off the fire. Add lemon juice or curd. Return to low heat, stir gently, till all the milk curdles and the greenish water called whey separates. Remove from fire. Leave it covered for 15 minutes. Strain through a muslin cloth and squeeze out all the whey.

If cubes of paneer are required, keep the paneer which is wrapped in the muslin cloth in a rectangular ice cream box or an aluminium ice tray. The paneer takes its shape. To get a compact brick of paneer, place a heavy weight on the paneer for an hour or so. Remove the cloth and use the perfect home made paneer even when it is not available in the market.

How to Prepare Khoya

Khoya is dried fresh whole milk. To prepare Khoya, boil 600 ml (3½ cups) of full cream milk in a heavy pan over quick fire and stir gently with a perforated spoon in the initial stage of drying. When the milk thickens, stir continuously and comparatively vigorously so that it does not stick to the bottom of the pan. Remove from the fire when it dries up and is converted into a single lump. Continue stirring till it stops sizzling.

It takes about 20 to 25 minutes to dry up 600 ml milk and it produces about 100 gms of Khoya.

Subz Shahjahani : Recipe on page 32 ➤

Weights and Measures

Use a tea cup for measuring.

A table spoon is written as tbsp, a teaspoon as tsp.

Food stuff	Measure	Weight (gms)
Cereals		
Rice	1 cup	125
Atta (wheat flour)	1 cup	100
Maida (plain flour)	1 cup	100
Suji	1 cup	120
Dals (Pulses)		
Average for all dals (pulses)	1/3 cup	50
Rajmah (kidney beans)	1 cup	125
Channa (chick peas)	1 cup	125
Besan (gram flour)	3/4 cup	50
Dairy Products		
Milk	1 cup	200
Milk powder	1/4 cup	20
Cheese grated	1 tbsp	5
Butter	1 cup	150
	1 tbsp	15
Curd (yoghurt)	1/2 cup	100
	1 tbsp	15
Cream	1/2 cup	100
	1 tbsp	15
Fats and Oils		
Refined oil	1 cup	125
	1 tbsp	10
Ghee (clarified butter)	1 cup	150
	1 tbsp	15

Food stuff	Measure	Weight (gms)
Nuts		
Ground nuts	1 tbsp (37 pieces)	10
	1/4 cup	40
Almonds	9 big	10
Cashewnuts	6 large	10
Walnuts	4 halves	10
Raisins	1 tbsp	10
Pista	1 tbsp (18 pieces)	10
Dessicated coconut	1/2 cup	25
Miscellaneous		
Tea leaves	1 tsp	1.5
Cocoa powder	1 tbsp	5
Coffee powder	1 tbsp	2
Custard powder	1 tbsp	6
Cornflour	1 tbsp	6
Creamed corn	1 tbsp	17
Gelatine	1 tbsp	5
Sugar	3/4 cup	100
Icing Sugar	1/4 cup	30
Vegetables		
Kheera (cucumber)	1 medium	150
Peas	10 Pods	50
French beans	13	50
Ginger	1" piece	10
Tomato	1 medium	50
Potato	1 medium	70
Onion	1 medium	60
Cauliflower	1 medium	400
Mushroom	7 medium	100
Cabbage	1 medium	400
Carrot	1 medium	60

Vegetarian Curries

Kaaju Matar Korma

PEAS & CASHEWNUTS IN A RICH GRAVY

Serves 4

½ cup kaju (cashewnuts)
1 tbsp kishmish (raisins)
½ cup boiled peas

GRAVY
3 onions - sliced finely
3 tomatoes - chopped
3 flakes garlic - chopped (optional)
1" piece ginger - chopped
2 tbsp magaz - tarbooz ke beej (watermelon seeds)
1 tbsp khus khus (poppy seeds) - soaked for ½ hour in warm water
1 tsp salt
½ tsp red chilli powder
½ tsp garam masala
½ cup milk

1. Shallow fry kajus in a little oil to a golden colour. Remove from oil. Keep aside.
2. Fry onions in the same oil till golden brown. Cool. Grind to a paste.
3. Mix tomatoes, garlic, ginger with 1 cup water in a small pan. Boil. Keep covered on low flame for 15 minutes till the tomatoes turn soft. Remove from fire. Cool. Grind to a puree. Keep puree aside.
4. Soak magaz and khus khus in ¼ cup water for ½ hour, otherwise it is difficult to grind the khus finely. Grind to a very fine paste.
5. Heat 2 tbsp oil. Add onion paste. Fry till golden brown.
6. Add red chilli powder. Mix for a few seconds.
7. Add the prepared tomato puree. Cook for 5-7 minutes till oil separates.
8. Add peas. Stir fry for 3-4 minutes. Add garam masala and salt.
9. Add magaz and khus paste. Stir for 2-3 minutes.
10. Add milk gradually, stirring continuously for 3-4 minutes on low flame.
11. Add enough hot water to get a thick gravy. Boil. Keep simmering on low flame for 7-8 minutes till oil separates.
12. Add the fried kaju and kishmish. Give one boil. Simmer on low flame for 3-4 minutes. Serve.

PANEER SHAHI

COTTAGE CHEESE IN MACE FLAVOURED TOMATO GRAVY

Picture on facing page | Serves 6

250 gms paneer (cottage cheese) - cut into 1" square, flat pieces

GRAVY

3 tbsp desi ghee or oil
2 onions - chopped
½" ginger - chopped
1 dry, red chilli - broken into bits
6-7 big tomatoes (500 gm) - chopped
¼ cup curd - beaten till smooth
2 tbsp cashewnuts soaked in a little water for 15 minutes and ground to a paste
¼ tsp crushed javetri (mace) - soaked along with cashewnuts
1½ tsp salt
½ tsp red chilli powder
3/4 tsp garam masala
½ tsp sugar (add according to sourness of tomatoes)
½ cup thin fresh cream (or milk, if cream is not available)
1 tbsp tomato ketchup

1. Grind soaked cashewnuts and javetri together to a fine paste.
2. Heat 2 tbsp ghee. Add onion, ginger and red chilli.
3. Cook on low flame until onions turn transparent. Add red chilli powder.
4. Add chopped tomatoes. Cover and cook for 7-8 minutes till the tomatoes turn pulpy. Add curd. Cook till the mixture turns red again.
5. Remove from fire. Cool.
6. Grind to a very smooth puree with ½ cup water in a mixer.
7. Heat 1 tbsp of ghee in a kadhai. Add the prepared tomato puree.
8. Stir fry for 3-4 minutes on low heat.
9. Add salt, garam masala, sugar and tomato sauce. Mix.
10. Add cashewnut paste. Cook on low flame for 1-2 minutes.
11. Add enough cream or milk to get the right consistency (thickness) of the gravy. Add paneer pieces.
12. Serve garnished with a swirl of cream, a few coriander leaves and ginger match-sticks.

Methi Roti : Recipe on page 90, Paneer Shahi ➤

Palak Kofta

STUFFED SPINACH BALLS IN GREEN GRAVY

Serves 6

750 gm palak (spinach) is the total amount required.

KOFTA

150 gm paneer - crumbled
250 gm paalak (spinach)
½ tsp salt, ¼ tsp red chilli powder
1 tbsp cornflour
2 slices bread - dipped in water and squeezed well

GRAVY

½ kg palak - chopped
2 onions , 1" piece ginger, 6-8 flakes garlic
2 tomatoes - pureed, 3/4 cup milk
½ tsp red chilli powder, ½ tsp salt or to taste, ¼ tsp pepper, ½ tsp garam masala
3 tbsp oil, 1 tsp full desi ghee

1. To prepare koftas, discard stems of paalak. Wash in plenty of water and pressure cook with ¼ cup water. Remove after the first whistle. Chop boiled paalak finely. Keep in a strainer for 10 minutes. Squeeze well. Mix paalak, paneer, bread, cornflour, red chilli powder and salt. Make balls. Roll in maida and deep fry.
2. To prepare the gravy, pressure cook ½ kg paalak with ¼ cup water to give one whistle. Keep on low flame for 4-5 minutes. Blend to a paste.
3. Blend the onions to a separate paste in a grinder.
4. Grind ginger and garlic to a paste. Blend tomatoes to a puree.
5. Heat oil in a big, deep kadhai. Add onion paste and stir fry till it turns rich brown in colour. Add tomatoes. Cook till dry.
6. Add chilli powder, garam masala and ginger-garlic paste. Cook on low flame for 5-7 minutes till it stops sticking to the bottom of the kadhai. Fry some more till it looks really well fried.
7. Add milk, stirring constantly. Cook till dry. Cook further till oil separates.
8. Add paalak. Add salt and pepper. Stir fry for 10 minutes till paalak looks well fried and turns thick.
9. Add koftas at the time of serving and heat for 1-2 minutes.
10. Heat ghee in a small pan. Remove from fire and add ½ tsp red chilli powder. Pour over the hot palak.

METHI MALAI MATAR

DRY FENUGREEK LEAVES & PEAS IN A THICK CREAMY GRAVY

Serves 4

1 cup shelled peas
½" stick dalchini (cinnamon)
2 moti illaichi (cardamom)
3-4 laung (cloves)
1 tbsp cashewnuts - soaked in ¼ cup warm water
2 tbsp oil
1 onion - grated
¼ tsp white pepper powder
½ cup (75 gms) malai (cream)
4 tbsp kasoori methi (dry fenugreek leaves)
salt to taste
½ tsp red chilli powder
a pinch of sugar
½ cup milk (approx)

1. Boil peas in salted water till tender.
2. Grind together dalchini, laung and seeds of moti illaichi. Keep aside.
3. Separately grind cashewnuts along with water to a smooth paste.
4. Heat oil. Add grated onions and cook on low heat till oil separates. Do not let the onions turn brown.
5. Add the freshly ground masala and pepper powder. Cook for a few seconds.
6. Add the kasoori methi and malai, cook on low heat for 2-3 minutes till malai dries up.
7. Add the boiled peas.
8. Add cashewnut paste and cook for a few seconds.
9. Add enough milk to get a thick gravy.
10. Add salt, sugar to taste and red chilli powder.
11. Serve garnished with a few boiled peas in the centre surrounded by a ring of cashewnut bits.

Palak Paneer

SPINACH WITH COTTAGE CHEESE

Serves 4

½ kg palak - remove stalks
2 onions - ground to a paste
1" piece ginger, 6-8 flakes garlic - ground to a paste
2 tomatoes - pureed
3/4 cup milk
½ tsp red chilli powder
½ tsp garam masala
½ tsp salt or to taste
¼ tsp pepper
3 tbsp oil
1 tsp full desi ghee
100 gm paneer (cottage cheese) - cut into 1" pieces and deep fried to a golden brown colour

1. Pressure cook paalak leaves with ¼ cup water to give one whistle. Keep on low flame for 4-5 minutes. Cool and blend to a paste in a grinder.
2. Blend the onions to a separate paste in a grinder.
3. Grind ginger and garlic to a paste.
4. Blend tomatoes to a puree.
5. Heat oil. Add onion paste and stir fry till rich brown in colour.
6. Add tomatoes. Cook till dry.
7. Add chilli powder, garam masala and ginger-garlic paste. Cook on low flame for 5-7 minutes till the tomatoes are well fried and dry.
8. Add milk, stirring constantly. Cook till dry and oil separates.
9. Add paalak. Add salt and pepper. Stir fry for 10 minutes till paalak looks well fried and turns thick.
10. Add fried paneer pieces. Cover and simmer on low flame for 3-4 minutes till paneer turns soft.
11. Heat 1 tsp ghee. Remove from fire. Add ½ tsp red chilli powder and pour over the hot paalak.

Mushroom Pea Curry

Serves 4

100 gms (½ packet) mushrooms - cut into halves
3/4 cup shelled peas
3½ tbsp oil
2 tbsp tomato puree
½ tsp garam masala
½ tsp red chilli powder
1 tsp dhania powder
1½ tsp salt or to taste
2 tbsp coriander leaves - chopped
1 tsp ginger paste

PASTE
2 big onions
2 tbsp cashewnuts
½ tsp shahi jeera (black cumin)
½ tsp ordinary jeera
2 laung (cloves)
1 green chilli
1 dry, red chilli

1. Grind the onions and the cashewnuts along with all the other ingredients of the paste with a little water to a fine paste.
2. Heat oil and fry the nut and onion paste to a rich golden colour, stirring continuously. Fry till rich brown in colour, sprinkling a little water now and then to prevent it from burning. Fry till oil separates.
3. Add tomato puree. Add garam masala, dhania powder and chilli powder. Stir for 2-3 minutes.
4. Add ginger paste. Stir for a minute.
5. Add ½ cup water. Boil. Add the mushrooms and peas. Stir fry for 4-5 minutes on low flame.
6. Add 1 cup of water and 1 tbsp coriander leaves. Add salt to taste. Cook covered on low flame, till the peas are done.
7. Remove from fire when the vegetables are cooked and the gravy is slightly thick.
8. Serve hot, garnished with well beaten dahi (a perfect substitute for cream) and ginger cut into thin match sticks.

Ratna Dum Aloo

SMALL WHOLE POTATOES IN A SPECIAL GRAVY

Picture on facing page *Serves 4*

(250 gm) 5 small sized or 8 baby potatoes
4 tbsp oil
3 large onions - sliced finely
1" piece ginger - chopped
3 tbsp magaz (watermelon seeds)
1 tbsp cashewnut pieces (tukra kaju)
3 tbsp ready made tomato puree
½ tsp dhania powder
3/4 tsp red chilli powder
3/4 tsp garam masala
1½ tsp salt or to taste
1 tsp tandoori masala

1. Peel potatoes. Cut into two equal halves if big or leave whole if baby potatoes are available.
2. Deep fry potatoes first on medium flame and then reduce the flame further and fry till they feel soft. Fry till golden brown. Remove from oil only when well cooked. Keep aside.
3. Soak magaz and kaju together in 2-3 tbsp water for 15 minutes. Grind to a fine paste.
4. Grind the onions and ginger to a paste. Keep onion paste aside.
5. Heat 4 tbsp oil. Add the onion paste. Stir for 5-7 minutes on low flame, till oil separates and onions turn golden brown.
6. Add the tomato puree. Cook for 2-3 minutes on low flame.
7. Add dhania powder, red chilli powder, garam masala and salt. Cook for a minute.
8. Add magaz-kaju paste. Cook for 2 minutes. Add enough water to get a thick gravy. Boil.
9. Add fried potatoes. Simmer on low heat for 5-7 minutes till potatoes are well cooked and coated with masala. Add tandoori masala.
10. Serve hot garnished with chopped coriander and magaz seeds.

Punjabi Kadhi

GRAMFLOUR DUMPLINGS IN A TANGY YOGHURT CURRY

Serves 4

1 cup besan (gram flour)
2 cups sour curd (yoghurt)
½ tsp haldi powder, 2½ tsp salt or to taste
3/4 tsp red chilli powder (according to taste)
2 tbsp oil
½ tsp jeera, 1 tsp rai (brown mustard seeds), ½ tsp methi seeds (fenugreek seeds)
3-4 dry, red chillies, 4-5 curry leaves

PAKORAS (DUMPLINGS)

1 big onion - chopped fine, 1 big potato - chopped fine
½" piece ginger - chopped fine, 2 green chillies - chopped fine
½ tsp red chilli pd, 1 tsp salt, ½ tsp garam masala, 1 tsp dhania pd.
a pinch of baking powder
1 cup besan
1/3 cup water
oil for frying

TEMPERING/BAGHAR

1½ tbsp oil
½ tsp jeera (cumin seeds), ¼ tsp red chilli powder

1. Mix curd, besan, salt, haldi, red chilli powder and 5½ cups water. Beat well till smooth and no lumps remain.
2. In a big heavy-bottomed pan, heat oil. Add jeera, rai and methi seeds.
3. When jeera turns golden, add dry red chillies and curry leaves. Fry 1 minute.
4. Add curd-water mixture. Stir continuously till it boils.
5. After one good boil, lower heat and simmer for 15 minutes. Keep aside.
6. To prepare pakoras, mix besan with water to make a paste. Beat well. Add all other ingredients given under pakoras. Beat well.
7. Heat oil and drop spoonful of batter. Deep fry pakoras to golden brown.
8. Add pakoras to the ready kadhi.
9. At serving time transfer the hot kadhi to a serving dish.
10. To temper the kadhi, heat oil in small pan. Reduce flame and add jeera.
11. When it turns golden, remove from fire and add red chilli powder. Pour on to the hot kadhi in the dish. Serve with boiled rice.

MIRCH MAKAI LAJAWAAB

Picture on cover *Serves 5-6*

10-12 pieces (150 gm) baby corns - cut lengthwise into 2 pieces
6 big green chillies - slit and deseeded
1 large onion - ground to a paste
2 tbsp cashews - soaked in warm water and ground to a paste
6 tbsp tomato puree
1" piece ginger - grated
4 tbsp oil
¼ tsp haldi
1 tsp dhania powder (ground coriander)
½ tsp garam masala
1¼ tsp salt, or to taste, ½ tsp red chilli powder
1 cup water
1 cup milk
½ cup cream (optional)

1. Heat 4 tbsp oil. Add green chillies and fry for 3-4 minutes till they turn slightly whitish. Remove from oil and keep aside.
2. Add baby corns and fry for 3-4 minutes till brown specs appear. Remove from oil and keep aside.
3. Heat the remaining oil. Add onion, fry till light brown.
4. Add haldi, dhania powder and garam masala. Stir for a minute.
5. Add tomato puree. Cook for 5 minutes on low heat till dry and oil separates.
6. Add cashew paste. Mix.
7. Add water and boil. Add salt and pepper to taste. Add fried baby corns. Simmer on low flame for 10 minutes.
8. Add ginger. Remove from fire and keep aside till serving time.
9. At serving time, keep the curry on low heat and add milk gradually, stirring continuously. Mix well and keep on low heat, stirring continuously till it just boils.
10. Add fried green chillies and cream. Remove from heat immediately and serve.

Note: Choose green chillies which are thick, big and light green, as the small, dark green ones are hotter. Remember, to deseed them. After deseeding them, tap them gently to remove all the seeds.

Bharwaan Kesari Kofte

STUFFED COTTAGE CHEESE BALLS IN SAFFRON GRAVY

Serves 6

KOFTAS (BALLS)

150 gms paneer (cottage cheese) - grated
2 small boiled potatoes - grated
2 slices of bread
½ tsp garam masala
½ tsp red chilli powder
salt to taste
2-3 tbsp maida (plain flour) - to coat

FILLING

1 small onion - very finely chopped
½ " piece ginger - very finely chopped
4-5 kaju - chopped
10-12 kishmish
¼ tsp each of salt, red chilli powder, garam masala

GRAVY

few strands kesar (saffron)
2 big onions
1" piece ginger
1 dry, red chilli
2 tej patta (bay leaf)
2-3 chhoti illaichi (green cardamom)
2 tbsp cashewnuts - soaked in ¼ cup warm water for 15 minutes and ground to a paste
3 tbsp tomato puree
2 tbsp desi ghee or 3 tbsp oil
½ tsp garam masala
½ tsp red chilli powder
1 tsp salt or to taste
½ cup fresh cream
½ cup milk mixed with ½ cup water

Continued.....

1. To prepare the koftas, mix grated paneer, potatoes, red chilli powder, salt and garam masala.
2. Cut sides of bread. Dip in water. Squeeze well. Add to the potato-paneer mixture. Mash well till smooth. Make 8-10 balls.
3. For the filling, heat 2 tsp oil. Add onion and ginger. Fry till golden brown. Add kaju, salt, garam masala and chilli powder. Remove from fire.
4. Flatten each ball of paneer mixture, put 1 tsp of onion filling and one kishmish in each ball. Form a ball again. Roll each ball in maida.
5. Deep fry 2-3 koftas at a time in hot oil. Keep aside.
6. To prepare the gravy, soak kesar in 1 tbsp warm water.
7. Grind onions, ginger and dry red chilli to a fine paste.
8. Heat 3 tbsp oil in a heavy bottomed karahi and add the onion paste. Add tej patta and chhoti illaichi. Cook on low flame till onions turn transparent and oil separates. Do not let the onions turn brown.
9. Add tomato puree. Cook for 1-2 minutes.
10. Add cashewnut paste. Cook for 1 minute. Add garam masala, red chilli powder and salt. Cook for 2 minutes.
11. Add milk mixed with water, to make a gravy. Boil. Simmer on low flame for 5 minutes. Add kesar, keeping aside a little for garnishing.
12. Add fresh cream. Mix well. Add a pinch of sugar if the gravy tastes a little sour. Remove from fire.
13. To serve, boil gravy. Add koftas. Keep on low heat for ½-1 minute. Serve immediately, sprinkled with cream and dotted with soaked kesar.

Dhingri Matar

Picture on facing page *Serves 4*

1 cup shelled peas
25 gms dhingri (dry white mushrooms) - washed and soaked overnight
3 medium sized tomatoes - blanched and pureed
4 tbsp oil
4 laung (cloves), 1 stick dalchini (cinnamon)
1 tsp salt, or to taste, ¼ tsp haldi powder
some chopped coriander

GRIND TO A PASTE TOGETHER
1" piece ginger, 6-7 flakes garlic
1 onion
2 red chillies (whole) - deseeded and soaked in water for 15 minutes

ROAST LIGHTLY ON A TAWA AND GRIND TO A POWDER
1 tbsp saboot dhania (coriander seeds)
seeds of 2 moti illaichi (brown cardamoms)
1 tsp jeera (cumin seeds)

1. Wash dhingri in 2-3 changes of water. Soak dhingri overnight. Next morning wash again in two changes of water. Cut dhingri into ½" pieces (small pieces) with a knife. Discard any very hard portion, if present.
2. Lightly roast on tawa - dhania, jeera and moti illaichi seeds. Cool and powder finely.
3. Put tomatoes in boiling water, remove the skin and puree.
4. Grind onion, garlic, ginger and soaked red chillies to a paste.
5. Heat oil in a pan. Add laung and dalchini. Wait for a minute.
6. Add ground onion masala paste, salt and haldi powder. Stir fry till onions turn brown and oil separates.
7. Add tomato puree. Cook till dry and oil separates.
8. Add dhingri to the fried masala and lower the heat and bhuno for 4-5 minutes.
9. Add peas and bhuno for another 1-2 minutes on low heat.
10. Add powdered dry masala of jeera, dhania and moti illaichi. Mix.
11. Add enough water (about 1½ cups) to get a gravy. Boil and simmer covered till peas get cooked and oil separates.

Mirch Ka Salan

CURRIED LARGE GREEN CHILLIES

Serves 4

250 gm large green chillies - slit lengthwise and deseeded
5 tbsp ground nuts - roasted
6 tbsp desiccated coconut
2 tbsp white til (sesame seeds)
8-10 curry leaves
¼ tsp haldi powder
1 tsp red chilli powder
1 tbsp jeera powder
1 tbsp dhania powder
½ tsp garam masala
1½ tsp salt
1 lemon sized ball of tamarind (imli) soaked in 1 cup hot water
4 tbsp oil

1. Dry roast in a kadhai, sesame seeds (til) and coconut till they change colour. Add groundnuts and grind to a fine paste. Use little water for grinding, if required.
2. Heat oil. Reduce flame. Add curry leaves. Fry for 1 minute.
3. Remove from fire. Add haldi, red chilli powder. Add jeera powder, dhania powder and salt. Return to fire. Fry for 1 minute.
4. Add til, coconut and groundnut paste, stirring continously on low flame. Fry for 1-2 minutes.
5. Add chillies. Fry for 1 minute. Add 2 cups water.
6. Lower heat and cover. Simmer for 5-7 minutes or till chillies are tender.
7. Squeeze tamarind water from soaked tamarind. Add to chillies. Give one boil.
8. Serve hot with boiled rice.

KHUMB MAKHANA

MUSHROOMS WITH PUFFED LOTUS SEEDS

Serves 6

200 gm mushrooms (preferably small in size)
3/4 cup (10 gm) makhana (puffed lotus seeds)
½ tsp jeera (cumin seeds)
2 small onions - chopped finely
1 tsp ginger paste, ½ tsp garlic paste
½ tsp saboot kali mirch (black peppercorns)
1/3 cup dahi (yoghurt) - beaten till smooth
1 tsp dhania pd, 3/4 tsp degi mirch, 1¼ tsp salt, ¼ tsp haldi
3 tbsp ready made tomato puree

POWDERED SPICES

1 chhoti illaichi (green cardamom) - powdered
1 moti illaichi (black cardamom) - powdered
¼ tsp javetri (mace) powder

1. Trim the stalk of mushrooms and wash mushrooms. Boil 3-4 cups water with 1 tsp salt and 2 tsp lemon juice. Soak mushrooms in it for 5-7 minutes.
2. Heat 4 tbsp oil in a kadhai. Add makhanas and shallow fry over medium heat for a minute or till they turn golden. Drain and reserve in a pan full of water until ready to cook.
3. Heat the left over oil. Reduce heat and add jeera and stir for ½ minute, or till it turns golden.
4. Add onions and cook till transparent. Add ginger and garlic paste and stir fry till onions are light golden. Add saboot kali mirch and stir for a few seconds.
5. Add whole mushrooms and stir fry for 5-7 minutes.
6. Add dahi. Stir fry till oil separates. Add dhania powder, degi mirch, salt and haldi. Stir for a minute.
7. Add tomato puree. Stir fry for 3-4 minutes. Add 1 cup water. Boil.
8. Drain soaked makhanas. Add to mushrooms.
9. Add the powdered spices also. Cover and simmer, stirring occasionally for 5-7 minutes, till you get the right consistency of the gravy. Serve.

SUBZ SHAHJAHANI

MIXED VEGETABLES IN A MUGHLAI GRAVY

Picture on page 11 Serves 4

½ of a small cauliflower - deep fried, ½ cup boiled or frozen peas
2 small carrots, 10-15 French beans

SHAHJAHANI PASTE

1 tbsp khus khus (poppy seeds), 2 chhoti illaichi (green cardamom) - crushed
2" piece fresh coconut - grated OR 1tbsp dessicated coconut (nariyal ka burada)
2 laung (cloves), 1 tej patta (bay leaf), 1 flower javetri (mace)

GRAVY

3 medium onions, 1" piece ginger, 1 cup curd - fresh
1 tsp salt or to taste, ½ tsp red chilli pd., ½ tsp garam masala, ½ cup milk, 4 tbsp oil

1. Scrape carrots and thread French beans. Chop carrots into ½ " cubes and cut French beans diagonally into ½" (slanting) pieces. Cut cauliflower into small florets and deep fry to a golden brown colour.
2. Heat 2 tbsp oil. Add beans and carrots. Cover and cook on low flame till done. Add ¼ tsp salt and garam masala.
3. To prepare the Shahjahani paste, heat 1 tsp oil in a heavy bottomed kadhai. Add khus khus, chhoti illaichi, coconut, laung, tej patta and javetri. Fry for 1 minute on a low flame, till the spices turn golden brown. Remove tej patta. Grind the fried spices to a very fine paste. Keep the Shahjahani paste aside.
4. Grind 3 onions and ginger to a paste in a blender. Heat 2 tbsp oil in a clean kadhai. Add the onion paste and cook till golden brown.
5. Reduce flame and add red chilli powder. Cook on low flame for 1-2 minutes more, till the onions turn brown and ghee separates. Beat fresh curd with a fork till smooth and add it gradually to the onion masala. Cook stirring continuously till masala turns brown again and the masala becomes thick.
6. Add the Shahjahani paste made with whole spices. Mix.
7. Add cooked peas, carrots and beans. Add salt to taste. Fry them in masala for 5 minutes. Add fried cauliflower.
8. Add 1 cup hot water and ½ cup milk. Boil.
9. Cook covered, for a few minutes till the vegetables are properly cooked and the masala coats the vegetables. Add a pinch of sugar if the curd added was a little sour.
10. Remove from fire. Serve.

MAWA MATAR

PEAS WITH DRIED WHOLE MILK

Serves 4

1 cup shelled peas
100 gms khoya (dried whole milk)
1 big onion
½" piece ginger
½ tsp jeera (cumin seeds)
2 green chillies
3 tbsp ready made tomato puree (Kissan or Godrej)
½ tsp red chilli powder
½ tsp garam masala
3/4 tsp salt or to taste
1 tbsp kishmish (raisins)
a few cashewnuts - optional
2 tbsp oil

1. Grind onions, ginger, jeera and green chillies with a little water to a paste.
2. Heat 2 tbsp oil. Add the onion-ginger paste. Cook on low heat till oil separates.
3. Add the tomato puree. Cook for 1-2 minutes.
4. Add red chilli powder and garam masala.
5. Add peas. Mix well. Add enough water to get a thick gravy. Add salt.
6. Cook covered till peas are done.
7. Grate khoya. Add khoya and mix lightly.
8. Add kishmish. Simmer on low flame for a few minutes.
9. Serve hot, garnished with grated khoya and cashewnuts.

Tandoori & Dry Vegetables

TANDOORI PANEER

ROASTED OR GRILLED COTTAGE CHEESE

Servings 4

250 gms paneer (cottage cheese) - cut into 1" thick pieces
2 capsicums - cut into fine rings
2 onions - cut into fine rings
2 tbsp ready made tomato puree
1 tsp lemon juice
1 tsp tandoori masala
2 tbsp oil

PASTE

1½" piece ginger
2-3 dry, red chillies
½ tsp jeera (cumin seeds)
3-4 flakes garlic - optional
½ tsp salt
¼ tsp red chilli powder
a pinch of haldi
½ tsp amchoor
½ tsp kala namak (rock salt)
2 tsp oil

1. Grind garlic, ginger, jeera and red chillies to a fine paste.
2. Add salt, chilli powder, haldi, kala namak and amchoor to the paste. Add oil also to the paste.
3. Cut paneer into 1" squares. Rub 3/4 of this paste on the paneer pieces. Marinate the paneer for at least 1 hour. Keep the left over paste aside.
4. Place the marinated paneer in a greased oven proof glass dish and grill for 15-20 minutes in a hot oven till the edges of the paneer pieces start getting slightly crisp. Remove from the oven and keep aside.
5. Heat 2 tbsp oil in a kadhai. Fry onion and capsicum rings for a few minutes till onions turn transparent.
6. Add the left over ginger paste and tomato puree. Stir fry for 2 minutes. Add lemon juice. Add ½ tsp salt. Mix.
7. Add paneer pieces. Sprinkle tandoori masala. Toss for 2 minutes.
8. Serve immediately.

Aloo Matar Masala

PEAS AND POTATOES SEASONED WITH CUMIN

Serves 4

1½ cups boiled or frozen peas
2 potatoes - boiled and each cut into four pieces
3 onions - cut into rings
½ tsp jeera (cumin seeds)
½ " piece ginger - chopped finely
2 green chillies - finely chopped
2 tomatoes - finely chopped
½ tsp garam masala
½ tsp amchoor
1 tsp dhania powder
1½ tsp tandoori masala
3/4 tsp salt or to taste
3 tbsp oil
1" piece ginger - cut into thin match sticks
2 tbsp chopped coriander

1. Deep fry big cubes of potato to a rich brown colour. Keep fried potatoes aside.
2. Heat oil. Add jeera. When it turns golden brown, add onion. Cook till onions turn light brown.
3. Add ginger and green chilli. Cook for 1 minute.
4. Add tomatoes. Cook for 5-7 minutes. Add dhania powder, red chilli powder, amchoor and garam masala. Stir fry for 2-3 minutes on low flame.
5. Add 3-4 tbsp water. Boil.
6. Add the peas. Add salt.
7. Cook, covered on low flame, stirring occasionally for 5-7 minutes, till peas are done.
8. Add the fried potatoes and tandoori masala. Cook on low flame for 4-5 minutes. Add 2-3 tbsp water. Mix.
9. Add ginger match sticks and chopped coriander. Stir fry and serve hot.

GOBHI TIKKA

CAULIFLOWER MARINATED IN GINGER-GARLIC PASTE & GRILLED

Serves 4

1 medium sized cauliflower - cut into big florets
2 onions - cut into rings
1" piece ginger - cut into match sticks
1 tbsp oil

MARINADE

1½ cups curd prepared from full cream milk - hung for 15 minutes in a muslin cloth
2 tsp oil
2 tsp garlic paste
2 tsp ginger paste
1 tsp salt
½ tsp kala namak (rock salt)
1½ tsp red chilli powder
1 tsp chaat masala
1 tsp black pepper
1 tsp amchoor

1. Cut cauliflower into big flowerets. Boil 4-5 cups of water with 1 tsp salt and 1 tsp lemon juice.
2. Add cauliflower. Boil for about 5 minutes till properly cooked, but do not over cook.
3. Strain. Keep in the strainer for 5 minutes to drain out all the water. Wipe with a clean kitchen towel.
4. Squeeze the hung curd. Mix all ingredients of the marinade with the hung curd.
5. Dip cauliflower pieces in this curd mixture. Marinate for ½ hour at least or more.
6. Grease the wire rack of the oven and arrange the cauliflower pieces on the wire rack, leaving the extra marinade behind. Place the rack in a hot oven and grill till it gets browned slightly. Keep aside.
7. Heat 1 tbsp oil in a kadhai at serving time. Saute onions rings and ginger match sticks in oil till onions turn transparent. Add the left over marinade. Mix. Add the grilled gobhi. Mix well and serve hot.

PALAK ALOO

SPINACH AND POTATOES FLAVOURED WITH CLOVES

Picture on facing page Serves 6

500 gm (1 small bundle) spinach (paalak)
2 small potatoes
1 " piece ginger - grated
3 tbsp oil or ghee
2 moti illaichi (black cardamoms)
1 " stick dalchini (cinnamon)
5-6 flakes garlic - crushed to a rough paste
2 onions - finely chopped
3 tomatoes - chopped
½ tsp haldi (turmeric powder)
1 tsp dhaniya powder (ground coriander)
½ tsp red chilli powder
½ tsp garam masala
1 tsp salt, or to taste

1. Wash and peel potatoes. Cut into 1" pieces. Cut away thick stalks of spinach. Chop leaves finely into thin strips or ribbons.
2. Heat oil. Reduce heat. Add moti illaichi and dalchini. Wait for a minute. Add garlic and cook till it starts to change colour.
3. Add onions and stir fry till golden. Reduce heat. Add haldi, dhania powder, chilli powder, garam masala and salt. Mix well on low heat for a minute.
4. Add ginger. Stir for a few seconds. Add tomatoes and stir fry for 3-4 minutes till well blended.
5. Add potatoes. Stir fry for 4-5 minutes. Cook covered for 10 minutes, sprinkling a little water occasionally, till the potatoes turn soft.
6. Add spinach. Continue cooking, without covering, for about 10 minutes, till the spinach gets wilted and is well blended with the potatoes.
7. Serve hot with paranthas or phulka.

MUSHROOMS IN YOGHURT

Serves 4

200 gms (1 packet fresh mushrooms)
2 tbsp oil
1 tsp ajwain (carom seeds)
2 onions - chopped finely
1" piece ginger
2 green chillies - chopped finely
1 tsp garam masala
3/4 tsp red chilli powder
1½ tsp dhania (coriander) powder
3/4 cup fresh curd - beaten well till smooth
salt to taste

1. Wash mushrooms thoroughly.
2. Cut the mushrooms in 'T' shaped slices. Each mushroom should be cut into 4-5 slices.
3. Heat oil in a non-stick pan. Add ajwain. Cook for ½ minute till it gets golden brown.
4. Add onions, green chillies and ginger. Cook till onions turn light brown in colour.
5. Add mushrooms. Cook covered, stirring occasionally, till mushrooms are done.
6. Add chilli powder and coriander powder. Stir for a few seconds.
7. Blend in beaten curd, garam masala and salt.
8. Cook till curd dries up and coats the mushrooms. Serve hot with chappatis.

Stuffed Capsicum

Serves 6-8 *Picture on back cover*

4 simla mirch (capsicums)
2 tbsp channa dal (split gram) - soaked in water for 15 minutes or more
3 potatoes - boiled and mashed roughly
2 onions - chopped finely
½ tsp jeera (cumin seeds)
½ tsp haldi powder, 1 tsp salt
1 tsp dhania (coriander) powder
¼ tsp amchoor (dried mango powder)
½ tsp garam masala, ½ tsp red chilli powder
1 tomato - pulp removed and finely chopped
2 tbsp hara dhania (fresh coriander) - finely chopped
2 tbsp oil

1. Cut a slice from the top of the capsicums. Scoop out the seeds and make it hollow. Rub a little salt on the inner surface. Keep them upside down for 10 minutes.
2. Boil channa dal in a little water for about 10 minutes, till very soft. Strain.
3. Heat 2 tbsp oil. Add jeera. When it turns golden, add chopped onion. Stir fry till light brown.
4. Add boiled dal. Stir fry for a minute. Reduce flame. Add haldi, dhania powder, amchoor, garam masala and chilli powder. Mix for a minute. Add pulp of tomato. Stir till it dries.
5. Add roughly mashed potatoes and salt to taste. Stir fry for 4-5 minutes till potatoes are well done. Add chopped coriander and pieces of tomato. Mix well.

4\. Fill the capsicums with this mixture. Press well and keep aside till serving time.

5\. Heat a non stick pan or a flat bottomed kadhai. Put 1 tbsp oil and spread the oil to coat the pan.

6\. Arrange the filled capsicum and cook covered on low heat for 8-10 minutes, changing the sides, till the capsicums get cooked. Do not cook for a longer time as they will turn limp on doing so. Remove from pan. Cut into two halves and serve.

7\. You may also cook the capsicums in the microwave or cook in a moderately hot oven.

KADHAI PANEER

COTTAGE CHEESE FLAVOURED WITH FENUGREEK

Serves 6

250 gms paneer (cottage cheese) - cut into long fingers
2 capsicums - cut into long fingers
2 dry, red chillies
1½ tsp saboot dhania (coriander seeds)
10-12 flakes garlic - crushed
1 green chilli - chopped
1½" piece ginger - chopped finely
1" piece ginger - finely shredded
2 tomatoes - chopped
a pinch of methi dana (fenugreek seeds)
1 tbsp kasoori methi (dry fenugreek leaves)
½ tsp salt
4 tbsp oil

1. Heat red chillies on a tawa, till slightly crisp and dry.
2. Roughly powder red chillies and saboot dhania together.
3. Heat 1 tbsp oil in a non-stick pan. Saute capsicums till done. Remove from pan and keep aside.
4. Heat 2 tbsp oil. Add crushed garlic. Fry till light brown. Add pounded dhania and red chillies. Cook for ½ minute.
5. Add chopped ginger and green chilli.
6. Add tomatoes, stir fry for about 5-7 minutes, on low heat till oil separates.
7. Add a pinch of methi dana and salt.
8. Add paneer and capsicum.
9. Sprinkle kasoori methi. Cook for 2-3 minutes.
10. Add shredded ginger. Mix well. Serve hot.

BHINDI LASOONI

OKRA SEASONED WITH GARLIC

Serves 4

250 gm bhindi (okra) - small and tender
4 tbsp oil

POWDERED SPICES
1 tsp salt
½ tsp red chilli powder
1 tsp dhania (coriander) powder
½ tsp garam masala
½ tsp haldi
1 tsp amchoor (dried mango powder)

OTHER INGREDIENTS
2 tsp garlic paste
1 tsp ginger paste
2 tbsp besan (gram flour)
½ tsp saunf (aniseeds)

1. Wash, drain bhindi.
2. Slice off ¼" from the top and the bottom of each bhindi. Make a slit in each piece. Keep the bhindi in a paraat or a large pan.
3. Mix all ingredients of the powdered spices together.
4. Sprinkle these mixed spices over the bhindi.
5. Add the ginger and garlic pastes. Rub well, so as to apply masala on all the bhindi pieces.
6. Sprinkle 1 tbsp besan, mix well with a spoon, so as to coat the bhindi. Sprinkle 1 more tbsp of besan and mix well. Marinate for 15 minutes.
7. Heat 5-6 tbsp oil. Add the bhindi.
8. Cook on low flame, stirring occasionally till it turns golden brown evenly. Cook till it is crisp and completely done.
9. Crush saunf and add to the bhindi. Cook for a few seconds. Serve hot.

PESHAWARI BHEIN

LOTUS STEMS SEASONED WITH CAROM SEEDS

Picture on facing page

Serves 4

250 gm thick bhein or kamal kakri (lotus stem)
1" piece ginger
4-5 flakes garlic
2 green chillies
½ tsp ajwain (carom seeds)
1 tsp lemon juice
1 tbsp curd
3/4 tsp salt
½ tsp red chilli powder
5-6 tbsp oil
2 tbsp besan (gram flour)
¼ tsp amchoor (dry mango powder)

1. Choose thick lotus stem (bhein). Cut bhein diagonally into ½" thick, slanting slices. Wash well. Use a toothpick to clean if it is dirty. Boil pieces in salted water till soft; or pressure cook in 1 cup water to give one whistle. Keep on low flame for 8-10 minutes.
2. Grind ginger, garlic, green chillies and ajwain to a paste.
3. Add lemon juice, curd, salt and red chilli powder to the above paste. Mix well.
4. Strain the boiled bhein. Wipe dry with a clean kitchen towel.
5. Apply the paste all over on the cooked bhein. Keep marinated bhein aside for 1 hour.
6. At serving time, heat 5-6 tbsp oil. Reduce flame. Add besan. Cook for ½ - 1 minute till the besan turns golden brown.
7. Add the marinated bhein and stir fry for 5-6 minutes on low flame till the besan coats the bhein.
8. Sprinkle some amchoor powder and garam masala. Stir fry for 2-3 minutes till they turn dry and crisp. Serve.

Note: At the time of buying bhein, see that both the ends are closed. The closed ends prevent the dirt from going inside.

Butter Nan : Recipe on page 89, Peshawari Bhein ➢

Saboot Gobhi

WHOLE CAULIFLOWER

Serves 6

2 very small whole cauliflowers
4 tbsp oil

MASALA
3 onions - sliced finely
3 tomatoes - roughly chopped
1" piece ginger - chopped
2 tbsp curd
½ tsp garam masala
½ tsp red chilli powder
½ tsp amchoor
salt to taste
¼ cup boiled peas - to garnish

1. Remove stem of cauliflowers. Boil 6-7 cups water in pan with 1 tsp lemon juice and 2 tsp salt. Add the whole cauliflowers. As soon as the water boils again, remove from fire. Keep soaked in water for 5 minutes. Strain. Wipe dry with a clean towel.
2. Heat 5-6 tbsp oil in a kadhai. Put one cauliflower with flower side down in oil. Cover and cook on medium flame, stirring occasionally till the cauliflower turns golden and gets cooked. Remove from oil. Fry the second cauliflower also and keep aside.
3. To prepare the masala, grind onions to a paste.
4. Heat ½ tbsp oil in a clean kadhai. Add the chopped tomatoes and ginger. Cook for 4-5 minutes till they turn soft. Remove from fire. Cool the tomatoes. Grind the cooked tomatoes to a paste.
5. Heat 3 tbsp oil in a kadahi. Add the onion paste, cook till onions turn brown.
6. Add cooked tomato paste. Cook for 3-4 minutes on low flame till masala turns dry.
7. Add well beaten curd. Cook till masala turns reddish again.
8. Add red chilli powder, amchoor and garam masala. Add salt to taste. Cook for 1 minute.

Continued ...

9. Add 2-3 tbsp water to get a thick, dry masala. Boil. Cook for 1 minute on low flame. Remove from fire.
10. Insert a little masala in between the florets of the fried cauliflower. Keep aside.
11. To serve, arrange the cauliflowers on a platter. Add 3-4 tbsp water to the masala to make it into a gravy. Boil. Pour over the arranged cauliflowers. Heat in a preheated oven.

    OR

    Heat 1 tbsp oil in a kadhai. Place the cauliflower. Cover and heat the whole flower on low heat till hot. Heat the masala separately by adding 2-3 tbsp water to make it into a gravy. Arrange the hot cauliflower on a serving platter. Pour the masala over it.
12. Sprinkle some boiled peas on it and on the sides. Serve.

Baghare Baingan

BRINJALS STUFFED WITH GROUND NUTS & SESAME SEEDS

Serves 4

250 gm (8-10 pieces) brinjals (small, round variety)
3/4 tbsp shakkar or gur (powdered jaggery)
1 tbsp roasted peanuts
1 tbsp fresh coriander leaves
3/4 tsp salt, ½ tsp red chilli powder, ¼ tsp garam masala
1 tsp ginger paste, 1 tsp garlic paste
4 tbsp oil
1 large onion - finely chopped
1 tsp full tamarind (a small marble sized ball) – soaked in ¼ cup warm water

ROAST TOGETHER

2 tsp freshly grated or dessicated (powdered) coconut
2 tsp til (sesame seeds), 2 tsp saboot dhania (coriander seeds)
½ tsp jeera (cumin seeds)

1. Wash and slit brinjals in fours leaving the stem intact. The brinjals should be whole with deep cuts.
2. Soak a small marble sized ball of tamarind in ¼ cup of warm water for a while. Rub to extract pulp and keep aside.
3. Roast coconut, til, jeera and coriander seeds on a tawa (griddle) on low flame till they just change colour.
4. Grind the roasted ingredients along with gur, roasted peanuts and coriander leaves together with 1 tbsp water to a fine paste.
5. Add salt, red chilli powder, garam masala, ginger and garlic to the above paste. Mix well. Fill this into the brinjals.
6. Heat oil. Reduce flame. Add 3-4 brinjals at a time on low flame. Fry till the skin turns brown and they turn soft. Keep all the fried brinjals aside.
7. Strain the left over oil. Heat oil and fry the chopped onion to a light golden colour. Add ¼ tsp of salt and ¼ tsp red chilli powder.
8. Add tamarind juice. Mix. Add brinjals, cover and cook for 5-7 minutes, on low heat, stirring occasionally taking care not to break the brinjals. Serve hot.

Chatpate Aloo

SPICY POTATOES PREPARED IN MUSTARD OIL

Serves 6-8

½ kg large potatoes - peeled and cut into thick fingers
mustard oil for frying potatoes
1½ tsp salt or to taste
1 tsp red chilli powder
1 tsp dhania powder
1 tsp bhuna jeera (roasted cumin seeds)
1 tsp amchoor
4 tsp white til (sesame seeds) - roasted on a tawa and ground to a powder
2 tbsp mustard oil
a small grain of hing (asafoetida)
2 green chillies - slit, deseeded and chopped
2 tbsp chopped coriander

1. Wash and peel the potatoes. Cut lengthwise into thick fingers.
2. Heat oil in a kadhai. When smoking hot, remove from fire and cool a bit. Put the kadhai with oil back on fire. Fry potatoes on medium fire till golden brown.
3. In an empty kadhai, mix salt, red chillies, dhania, jeera, til and amchoor.
4. Add potatoes, green chillies and coriander. Mix well. Keep aside.
5. Heat 2 tbsp mustard oil to smoking point in a separate small vessel.
6. Add hing. Stir for ½ minute.
7. Pour the oil on to the potatoes in the kadhai. Toss for a few minutes on fire.
8. Serve with chappatis or even as a snack.

Tawa Mushrooms

MUSHROOMS FLAVOURED WITH CORIANDER SEEDS

Picture on facing page　　　　Serves 4

200 gm (1 packet) fresh mushrooms - small sized
1 capsicum - cut into 1" pieces
2 onions - finely chopped
½" piece ginger
5-6 flakes garlic
3 tomatoes - chopped finely
2 dry, red chillies
1 tbsp saboot dhania (coriander seeds)
a pinch of methi dana (fenugreek seeds)
2 tsp kasoori methi (dry fenugreek leaves)
3/4 tsp salt or to taste
2 green chillies - cut into thin long strips
1" piece ginger - grated into long shreds
5 tbsp oil

1. Grind ginger and garlic to a paste.
2. Grind together red chillies and saboot dhania to a coarse powder.
3. Wash mushrooms well in water to remove any dirt.
4. Remove the base of the stem of the mushrooms. If mushrooms are small, keep them whole, if big, cut into halves.
5. Boil 4-5 cups water with 2 tsp lemon juice and 1 tsp salt. Remove from fire. Soak the mushrooms in it for 5 minutes. Drain.
6. Heat 3 tbsp oil. Add drained mushrooms. Cook, stirring, for 7-8 minutes till they turn brown and get cooked properly.
7. Add capsicum. Cook on medium flame for 3-4 minutes. Remove mushrooms and capsicum from oil.
8. Heat 2 tbsp oil. Add chopped onions. Cook till light brown.
9. Add ginger-garlic paste. Cook for ½ minute. Add dhania-chilli pd.
10. Add chopped tomatoes. Cook for 7-8 minutes, till oil separates.
11. Add methi dana and salt. Cook for ½ minute. Add ¼ cup water.
12. Add cooked mushrooms and capsicum. Mix. Add kasoori methi. Stir-fry for 2-3 minutes. Remove from fire. Garnish with slit green chillies and shredded ginger.

Paneer Tikka

Picture on page 2

Serves 4

300 gm paneer - cut into 1½" squares of 3/4" thickness
1 large capsicum - deseeded and cut into 1" pieces (12 pieces)
1 onion - cut into 4 pieces and then separated

MARINADE

¼ cup drained thick dahi (yogurt) - (hang ½ cup yogurt for 15 minutes)
2 tbsp thick malai or thick cream
a few drops of orange colour or a pinch of turmeric
2 tbsp oil
1 tbsp (level) cornflour
½ tsp amchoor
½ tsp kala namak, 3/4 tsp salt, or to taste
1 tbsp tandoori masala

GRIND TOGETHER

1" piece ginger, 5-6 flakes garlic
2 dried, whole red chillies - soaked for 10 minutes

1. Drain soaked red chillies. Grind ginger, garlic and red chillies to a paste.
2. To the ginger-garlic-chilli paste, add hung dahi, cream, 2 tbsp oil, 1 tbsp cornflour, amchoor, salt, kala namak, tandoori masala and colour or haldi.
3. Brush a grill rack or skewers generously with oil.
4. Dip each paneer piece in the marinade and toss well to coat all sides. Arrange on the rack or on the skewers. After all the paneer pieces are done, put the capsicum and onions - both together in the left over marinade and mix well to coat the vegetables.
5. Transfer to a greased oven proof tray. Keep aside the marinated paneer, capsicum and onion for at least 1 hour.
6. At the time of serving, put the paneer pieces first. Grill till almost done, for about 15 minutes. Grill the paneer till it gets dry and starts getting crisp.
7. Remove from grill and baste (sprinkle some oil) paneer with some oil. Now put the paneer and the vegetables in a tray, in the oven and grill everything for another 5 minutes. The vegetables should not be grilled for too long. Remove from the oven.
8. Serve really hot, sprinkled with some lemon juice and chaat masala.

Anokhi Arbi

ROASTED COLOCASIA FLAVOURED WITH CAROM SEEDS

Serves 4

½ kg arbi (colocasia) - medium size
1 cup curd (prepared from full cream milk) - hung for ½ hour
1 tbsp tandoori or chaat masala
few drops of orange colour - optional
4-5 onions - thinly sliced
½" piece ginger - shredded
1½ tsp saboot dhania (coriander seeds) - crushed to a rough powder
½ tsp garam masala
4-5 tbsp oil
1½ tsp amchoor
3-4 green chillies - slit lengthwise
¼ tsp salt
½ tsp ajwain (carom seeds)

1. Peel arbi. Cut into two pieces.
2. Hang curd in a muslin cloth for ½ hour.
3. Boil arbi in salted water with ½ tsp of amchoor, for 10-12 minutes. Wash thoroughly. Keep in a strainer till all the water drains out completely.
4. Mix tandoori masala or chaat masala to curd. Add a few drops of orange colour if desired.
5. Grease an oven proof glass dish. Dip arbi pieces in the prepared curd and arrange in the dish.
6. Keep in a hot oven for ½ hour till the curd dries up and forms a coating. Keep aside.
7. Heat oil. Add ajwain. Stir till golden.
8. Add sliced onions. Cook till light brown.
9. Add all spices and salt. Add the grilled arbi.
10. Add the shredded ginger and green chillies. Mix well.
11. Fry the arbi, stirring continuously for 5 minutes, adding a few tsp of oil, if it sticks to the kadhai.
12. Remove from fire. Serve hot.

Achaari Karela

BITTER GOURD STUFFED WITH PICKLED ONION

Serves 6-7

½ kg (10-12) karelas (bitter gourd) with stalks - medium size
3 onions - chopped
¼ tsp methi dana (fenugreek seeds)
¼ tsp kalaunji (onion seeds)
1 tsp saunf (aniseeds)
3/4 tsp salt
2 tsp amchoor
½ tsp red chilli powder
½ tsp garam masala
½ tsp dhania powder
4 tbsp oil

1. Peel karelas, keeping the stalks intact. Slit. Remove all seeds if they are hard, if not too hard, remove some to make place for the stuffing.
2. Rub salt inside and on the surface of karelas. Keep aside for at least 1 hour or even over night in the refrigerator.
3. Heat 1 tbsp oil. Add methi dana, kalaunji and saunf. Fry till saunf changes colour.
4. Add onions and fry till light brown.
5. Add salt, amchoor, red chilli powder, garam masala and dhania powder. Cook and mash the onions for 1-2 minutes on fire. Remove from fire. Keep aside.
6. Squeeze the karelas, wash a few times in water.
7. Boil 3 cups water with 2 tsp salt. Add karelas and boil, covered, on low flame for 7-8 minutes, till the karelas feels soft when a knife is inserted in them. Drain. Cool.
8. Fill 1 tbsp of onion stuffing in each karela. Tie a thread loosely over the karelas.
9. Heat 3 tbsp oil in a flat bottomed kadhai. Add karelas. Cook on medium fire, stirring occasionally. Cook till karelas are done and evenly browned. Serve.

Mixed Vegetables

Serves 4

2 carrots
150 gms French beans
4 onions - cut into rings
½ cup shelled peas - (optional)
1" piece ginger - grated
2 green chilies - chopped
3 tomatoes - chopped
½ tsp haldi power
½ tsp garam masala
1 tsp dhania powder
½ tsp red chilli powder
1 tsp tandoori masala
2 laung (cloves) - crushed to a powder
3 tbsp oil

1. Peel carrots. Divide into two lengthwise. Cut slices in a slanting manner (diagonal slices).
2. Thread French beans. Cut into ½" diagonal slices.
3. Heat oil. Add onions and cook till transparent.
4. Add ginger and green chillies. Cook for 1 minute. Add haldi powder. Mix.
5. Add tomatoes and cook for 3-4 minutes.
6. Add garam masala, dhania powder and red chilli powder. Cook till oil separates.
7. Add beans, carrots and peas. Stir fry for 3-4 minutes. Cover and cook on low flame till vegetables are done.
8. Add tandoori masala and powdered laung. Mix well. Serve hot.

Makhani Arbi

COLOCASIA IN A SEMI DRY BUTTER GRAVY

Serves 4

250 gm arbi (colocasia) of medium size
2 tbsp besan (gram flour)
½ tsp ajwain (carom seeds)
1 onion - chopped
1 green chilli - slit, deseeded and chopped
½ tbsp grated ginger
1 tbsp chopped coriander
½ tsp salt or to taste, ½ tsp red chilli powder, ¼ tsp garam masala
½ tbsp lemon juice

GRAVY

250 gm (3-4) tomatoes - chopped roughly
½ tsp ginger paste, ½ tsp garlic paste
1 green chilli
2 laung (cloves)
1 chhoti illaichi (green cardamom)
salt to taste, ½ tsp red chilli powder
2 tbsp butter
1 tsp honey
1 tbsp kasoori methi

1. Pressure cook whole arbi with 3 cups water to give one whistle. Keep on low flame for 2-3 minutes. Remove from fire. Cool and drain.
2. To prepare makhani gravy, cook tomatoes in a heavy bottomed pan with 1 cup water, ginger and garlic paste, green chilli, red chilli powder, laung, chhoti illaichi. Boil. Cover and cook on low heat till it is reduced to a saucy consistency.
3. Remove from fire. Blend in a mixer. Strain into a clean pan.
4. Add butter. Stir in honey.
5. Add salt to taste. Keep on fire. Boil. Simmer on low flame for 1-2 minutes.
6. Add kasoori methi and remove from fire. Keep makhani gravy aside.
7. Peel and flatten each piece of arbi. Sprinkle some salt and red chilli powder on it. Sprinkle dry besan. Over turn the pieces and sprinkle salt, red chilli and besan on the other side too. Mix, so as to coat lightly.

Continued.....

8. Heat some oil in a pan, add shallow fry the arbi over medium heat till golden.
9. Heat 2 tbsp oil in a clean pan. Add ajwain. When it turns golden, add chopped onions, grated ginger and green chillies and saute for 3 minutes. Add ½ tsp salt.
10. Add the arbi. Add red chillies and ½ of the coriander. Stir fry for a minute.
11. Add the prepared makhani gravy and stir fry until the arbi is coated with the gravy.
12. Adjust seasoning. Sprinkle lemon juice, garam masala and the remaining coriander.
13. Stir well and serve immediately.

Balti Aloo

POTATOES WITH MUSTARD & FENNEL

Serves 4

4 medium potatoes - cut into ¼" thick round slices
2 medium onions - sliced
3 tbsp oil
½ tsp jeera (cumin seeds)
½ tsp saunf (fennel)
2 pinches kalaunji (onion seeds)
2 pinches rai (mustard seeds)
a pinch methi dana (fenugreek seeds)
2 dried, red chillies - crushed
4 flakes garlic - crushed
½" piece ginger - cut into thin match sticks
a few curry leaves
½ tsp haldi
salt to taste
1 tsp chaat masala
1 tbsp coriander - chopped
1 fresh red chilli - deseeded and cut into thin match sticks
1 green chilli - deseeded and cut into thin match sticks

1. Peel, wash and cut potatoes into ¼" thick round slices.
2. Heat oil in a kadhai or a non stick wok.
3. Reduce heat slightly, add jeera, saunf, kalaunji, rai and methi dana. Fry for ½ minute till the saunf starts changing colour.
4. Add garlic, ginger, red chillies and curry leaves, stir fry for 1 minute.
5. Add onions, cook until onions turn light golden. Add haldi. Stir.
6. Add potatoes and salt. Mix well.
7. Add coriander, fresh red and green chillies, stir until well mixed.
8. Reduce to very low heat, cover tightly with a lid, and cook for 10-12 minutes or until the potatoes are tender. Uncover and add chaat masala. Adjust the seasonings.
9. Transfer to a serving platter and serve hot.

KASTOORI GAJAR MATAR

PEAS & CARROTS FLAVOURED WITH FENUGREEK

Serves 4

1 packet (2 cups) kasoori methi (dried fenugreek leaves) - cleaned and soaked in water for ½ hour
1 cup milk
1½ cups shelled peas - boiled
3 carrots - cut into ¼" cubes (1½ cups chopped)
2 tbsp mustard oil or any refined oil
1 tsp salt
½ tsp red chilli
½ tsp garam masala
a pinch of amchoor (dried mango powder)
a pinch of sugar

1. Soak cleaned methi in water for at least ½ hour or even more. Strain the methi and keep aside.
2. Heat oil in a heavy bottomed or a non stick kadhai.
3. Add methi and milk. Cook till completely dry. Add sugar. Mix well.
4. Add salt and red chilli powder. Cook for 1 minute.
5. Add carrots. Stir fry for 1-2 minutes on low flame.
6. Cover and cook, sprinkling a little water in-between, on low flame till the carrots are done.
7. Add boiled peas. Add garam masala and amchoor.
8. Uncover the vegetables and stir fry for 2-3 minutes.
9. At serving time, add ¼ cup milk and heat the vegetable well.

BHEIN MIRCH MASALA

HOT & SPICY LOTUS STEM

Serves 4-6

300 gms (2 medium pieces) lotus stem (bhein) - peeled and cut into ¼" thick slices
3 tbsp oil
2 onions - finely chopped
1" piece ginger - chopped
2-3 green chillies - deseeded & chopped
8-10 flakes garlic - crushed
3/4 cup curd - well beaten
2 tomatoes - chopped
3/4 tsp salt, ½ tsp garam masala,½ tsp amchoor

SABOOT GARAM MASALA
1 moti illaichi, 2-3 laung (cloves)
1" stick dalchini (cinnamon), ½ tsp jeera (cumin seeds)

MIRCH MASALA (POWDER TOGETHER ROUGHLY)
2 whole, dry red chillies
1 tsp dhania saboot (coriander seeds)
½ tsp saboot kali mirch (pepper corns)
¼ tsp shahi jeera (black cumin seeds)

1. Boil 4-5 cups water with 2 tsp salt and 2 tsp lemon juice. Add bhein. Cover and simmer on low flame for about 15 minutes, till well done. Drain and keep aside.
2. Heat oil in a kadhai. Reduce flame and add all the saboot garam masalas. Wait for ½-1 minute till jeera turns golden.
3. Add onions. Stir till light brown. Add ginger and green chillies.
4. Add the freshly powdered mirch masala.
5. Add garlic and stir fry for another minute.
6. Beat curd and add to the onions, stirring continuously. Stir fry for 5-7 minutes, till oil separates.
7. Add chopped tomatoes, salt, ½ tsp garam masala, ½ tsp amchoor and stir fry till oil separates.
8. Add ½ cup water. Boil. Add boiled pieces of bhein. Stir fry for 5-7 minutes. Cover and simmer on low flame for 10 minutes. Serve hot.

Aloo Nazaakat

POTATOES COATED WITH SESAME SEEDS

Serves 4

4 small sized potatoes or 8 round, baby potatoes
2 tsp til (sesame seeds)
3 tbsp oil
½ tsp jeera (cumin seeds)
1 onion - chopped finely
8-10 kajus
10-15 kishmish - soaked for 10 minutes
3/4 cup boiled or frozen peas
3/4 tsp salt or to taste
½ tsp haldi
½ tsp garam masala
½ tsp red chilli powder
¼ tsp amchoor
2 tbsp chopped coriander
2 green chillies - slit lengthways

1. Boil potatoes in salted water until just tender. They should feel soft when a knife is inserted. Do not over cook. Peel and cut each potato into 2 equal halves. Leave whole if baby potatoes are available.
2. Dry roast til on a tawa on low flame, until golden brown. Keep aside.
3. Heat oil. Add jeera. When it splutters and turns golden, add onions. Cook until onions turn transparent.
4. Add kaju. Stir-fry till golden. Add boiled peas and kishmish.
5. Add salt, garam masala, red chilli powder, amchoor, haldi, green chillies and fresh coriander. Cook for 1 minute.
6. Add the potatoes. Stir-fry gently for about 3 minutes, taking care not to break the potatoes.
7. Finally, sprinkle til, keeping aside a little for garnishing. Mix gently so that the potatoes are well coated. Remove from fire.
8. Sprinkle some more til on the aloos at the time of serving.

Pulses & Lentils

Arhar Dal with Paalak

SPINACH WITH LENTILS

Serves 4

3 cups (250 gm) chopped paalak (spinach)
1 cup arhar dal or toovar ki dal (red gram dal)
1 flake garlic - finely chopped (optional)
½ " piece ginger - finely chopped
1 green chilli - finely chopped
½ tsp haldi (turmeric powder)
1½ tsp salt or to taste
1 tsp oil

BAGHAR (TEMPERING)
3-4 tbsp oil or desi ghee
½ tsp ghee
1 onion - chopped finely
1 tomato - chopped finely
½ tsp garam masala, ½ tsp dhania powder, 1/8 tsp amchoor
½ tsp red chilli powder
1 green chilli - cut lengthways into 4 pieces

1. Pick, clean and wash dal. Wash chopped paalak in plenty of water.
2. Mix dal, paalak, garlic, ginger, green chilli, haldi, salt and oil. Add 3 cups water to the dal.
3. Pressure cook dal to give one whistle and then keep on low flame for 6-7 minutes. Remove from fire. Keep aside.
4. To prepare the baghar, heat oil or ghee in a clean kadhai.
5. Reduce heat. Add jeera. When it turns golden brown, add onions.
6. Stir fry the onions till they are rich brown in colour.
7. Add tomatoes. Cook on low flame for 2-3 minutes.
8. Add garam masala, dhania powder and amchoor. Cook for ½ minute.
9. Remove from fire and add green chillies and red chilli powder. Mix well.
10. Pour over the hot dal. Mix gently. Serve hot.

DAL MAKHANI

CREAMY SPLIT BLACK BEANS

Picture on facing page

Serves 6

1 cup urad saboot (whole black beans)
2 tbsp channe ki dal (split gram dal)
2 tbsp rajmah (kidney beans) - optional - soaked for at least 6 hours or overnight
1 tbsp ghee or oil
5 cups of water
1½ tsp salt
4 tomatoes - pureed in a mixer
3 tbsp ghee or oil
2 tsp dhania (coriander) powder
½ tsp garam masala
1 tsp tomato ketchup
1 tbsp butter
100 gm (½ cup) fresh cream
1" piece ginger, 4 flakes garlic (optional), 2 dry red chillies - grind together to a paste

1. Clean, wash dals. I f you want to add rajmahs, soak both dals and rajmah together in a pressure cooker for 6 hours.
2. Discard water and add 5 cups fresh water.
3. Pressure cook both dals and rajmah with 1 tbsp ghee, salt and half of the ginger-garlic paste. Keep the left over paste aside.
4. After the first whistle, keep on low flame for 40 minutes. Remove from fire. Keep aside.
5. Heat ghee. Add tomatoes pureed in a grinder. Cook until it turns thick.
6. Add the left over ginger paste, garam masala and coriander pd. Cook until ghee separates.
7. Add this tomato mixture to the boiled dal. Add tomato ketchup and butter.
8. Simmer on low flame for 8-10 minutes, stirring and mashing the dal occasionally.
9. Add enough cream to get the right colour and smoothness. Simmer for 1-2 minutes more. Remove from fire. Serve hot.

PANCHRATNI DAL

FIVE PULSES COOKED TOGETHER

Serves 4

3 tbsp urad dhuli dal (split black beans)
3 tbsp arhar dal (red gram dal)
3 tbsp channe ki dal (split gram)
3 tbsp moong dhuli dal (split green beans)
3 tbsp saboot masoor dal (lentil)

BAGHAR
3 tbsp oil
1 tsp rai (mustard seeds)
1 tsp jeera (cumin seeds)
2 laung (cloves)
½" stick dalchini (cinnamon)
few curry leaves
2 dry , red chillies - broken into bits
2 green chillies - chopped
½" ginger piece - chopped
3 tomatoes - chopped
½ tsp garam masala
1 tbsp chopped coriander
juice of ½ lemon

1. Clean, wash all dals. Pressure cook together with 3½ cups of water and 1½ tsp of salt.
2. After the first whistle, keep on low flame for 5-7 minutes.
   Remove from fire. Keep aside.
3. For the baghar, collect mustard seeds, jeera, dalchini and laung together.
4. Heat oil. Reduce heat. Add the collected jeera etc. Cook for a few seconds. Add ginger, curry leaves, red and green chillies. Fry for a few seconds.
5. Add the tomatoes and garam masala and cook for 1-2 minutes. Add this baghar to the dal. Add chopped coriander also.
6. Bring dal to boil, keep on low flame for 2-3 minutes.
7. Add lemon juice. Mix well. Serve hot.

Sambhar

MIXED VEGETABLES IN SOUR LENTILS

Serves 4

1 cup mixed vegetables - mooli (radish), onion, potato, bhindi (ladies finger), brinjal, capsicum - cut into ½ " pieces
2 green chillies - slit lengthways
½ cup arhar dal (red gram)
3 tsp sambhar powder
½ tsp haldi (turmeric powder)
1 tbsp rice flour - optional
lemon-sized ball of imli (tamarind)
salt to taste
1 small bunch chopped coriander leaves for garnishing

BAGHAR
2 tbsp oil
½ tsp sarson (mustard seeds)
¼ tsp hing (asafoetida) powder
¼ tsp methi dana (fenugreek seeds)
½ tsp jeera (cumin seeds)
1 dry, red chilli
a few curry leaves

1. Pressure cook dal with 2 cups of water till well blended.
2. Soak imli in 1 cup of hot water and extract pulp.
3. Heat oil. Add all the ingredients of the baghar. When the mustard seeds splutter, add the slit green chillies and the chopped vegetables. Fry for 3-4 minutes.
4. Add the imli pulp, salt, haldi and sambhar powder. Cover and simmer on a low heat till the vegetables are tender.
5. Add the cooked dal and simmer for 5 minutes till everything blends.
6. If the sambhar needs to be thickened, make a smooth paste of the rice flour in 2 tbsp of water and add to the sambhar and cook for another 2-3 minutes, till the raw smell disappears.
7. Garnish with chopped coriander leaves. Serve hot with rice.

DAL PALAK

SPLIT GRAMS WITH SPINACH

Serves 4

½ cup channe ki dal (split gram)
½ kg palak (spinach)
3 tbsp oil
1 onion - chopped
2 tomatoes - chopped
1-2 green chillies - chopped
½ " piece ginger - chopped
1 tsp dhania (coriander) powder
½ tsp garam masala
½ tsp red chilli powder

1. Soak dal for ½ hour.
2. Wash, chop palak leaves. Discard the stems.
3. Heat oil in a pressure cooker. Fry chopped onion till golden brown.
4. Strain the soaked dal. Add dal, palak and all other ingredients, including the spices into the pressure cooker. Stir fry for 1 minute.
5. Add ¼ cup water.
6. Pressure cook to give 2 whistles, then cook on low heat for 8-10 minutes. Remove from fire.
7. After the pressure comes down, mash the dal slightly.
8. Serve hot with boiled rice or rotis.

Channa Masala

SPICED CHICK PEAS

Serves 4

CHANNA MASALA
1 cup channa kabuli (Bengal gram)
2 tbsp channe ki dal (split gram)
2 moti illaichi (big cardamom)
1" stick dalchini (cinnamon)
2 tsp tea leaves tied in a muslin cloth or a tea bag
¼ tsp mitha soda (soda bicarb)
1" piece ginger - chopped finely
1 green chilli - chopped finely
1½ tsp anardana (pomegranate seeds) powder
2 onions - chopped finely
1 big tomato - chopped finely
½ tsp garam masala
1 tsp channa masala, 1 tsp dhania powder
salt and red chilli powder to taste

1. Soak channa channe ki dal with moti illaichi, dalchini, tea leaves, ¼ tsp soda, and enough water, overnight or for 6-8 hours in a pressure cooker.
2. Pressure cook all the ingredients together to give one whistle. After the first whistle, keep on low flame for about 20 minutes. Keep aside.
3. Heat 4 tbsp oil. Add onions. Saute till transparent. Add anardana powder. Cook stirring till onions turn dark brown. (Do not burn them). Add chopped tomatoes, ginger, green chilli. Stir fry for 3-4 minutes.
4. Add dhania powder and garam masala. Mash stir fry tomatoes occasionally till they turn brownish in colour and oil separates.
5. Add red chilli powder.
6. Remove tea bag and the whole spices from the boiled channas and add to the onion-tomato masala. Mix well. Add salt. Cook for 5-7 minutes.
7. Add channa masala. Mix well. Keep on low flame for 10-15 minutes.
8. At serving time, heat 2 tbsp oil on a tawa. Toss 1 tomato cut into 2 halves and 1 green chilli slit lengthways; for a few seconds in it. Shut off the flame.
9. Add ½ tsp red chilli powder and pour over the hot channas in the serving dish.

Masala Masoor

LENTILS SEASONED WITH GARLIC

Serves 4

1 cup saboot masoor (lentil)
1 big onion - sliced finely
2 large tomatoes - chopped
4-6 small whole onions
2 tbsp ghee
1½ tbsp chopped coriander

PASTE
4 flakes garlic
2 dry, red chillies
2 tsp dhania saboot (coriander seeds)
1 tsp jeera (cumin seeds)
1½" piece ginger

1. Pick, clean wash masoor.
2. Add 5 cups water and the whole onions.
3. Pressure cook for 10-12 minutes on low flame after the first whistle. Keep aside.
4. Grind all ingredients of the paste together. Keep garlic-chilli paste aside.
5. Heat ghee in a karahi. Add sliced onions. Fry for 3-4 minutes till they turn brown.
6. Add garlic-chilli paste to the onions. Cook for 2-3 minutes on low flame.
7. Add the cooked masoor and salt. Keep on low flame for 5 minutes.
8. Add tomatoes. Cook for 10 minutes.
9. Serve hot, sprinkled with chopped coriander.

RAJMAH

KIDNEY BEANS IN TOMATO GRAVY

Serves 6

1½ cups lal rajmah (red kidney beans)
1 tbsp channe ki dal (split gram)
2 tsp salt or to taste
1 onion - chopped finely
6-8 flakes garlic - crushed, 1" piece ginger - chopped finely
4 tbsp oil
3 tomatoes - pureed in a blender
½ cup curd - beaten well with a spoon
3 tsp dhania (coriander) powder
½ tsp garam masala, ½ tsp chilli powder (or to taste)
¼ tsp amchoor (dry mango powder)
2 tbsp chopped fresh coriander
2 laung (cloves) - powdered roughly

1. Wash and soak rajmah and dal in 4-5 cups of water overnight, or for at least 4-6 hours in a clean pressure cooker.
2. Drain the water. Add fresh 5 cups water. Add salt, chopped onion, garlic and ginger. Pressure cook to give one whistle. Keep on low flame for ½ hour. Remove from fire.
3. Heat 4 tbsp oil in a heavy bottomed kadhai. Add tomatoes pureed in a blender. Cook till tomatoes turn dry.
4. Reduce flame and add dhania powder, garam masala, red chilli powder and amchoor. Cook till oil separates.
5. Add beaten curd and stir continuously on low flame till the masala turns red again and oil separates.
6. Add powdered laung.
7. Strain and add the rajmahs, keeping the water aside. Stir fry on low flame for 5-7 minutes, mashing occasionally. Add the water of the rajmahs and cook for 10- 15 minutes till well blended.
8. Add the coriander leaves and mix well. Serve hot with chappatis or boiled rice.

SUKHI URAD DAL

A DRY PREPARATION OF SPLIT BLACK BEANS

Serves 4

1 cup dhuli urad (split black beans) - soaked for 20 minutes
1 tbsp oil
½ tsp haldi
1¼ tsp salt
½ tsp jeera (cumin seeds)
¼ tsp garam masala (mixed spices)
¼ tsp dhania (coriander) powder
¼ tsp red chilli powder

BAGHAR
3 tbsp oil
1 onion - sliced finely
¼ tsp red chilli powder
1 tsp shredded ginger - to garnish
1 tbsp chopped coriander - to garnish

1. Strain the soaked dal and keep aside.
2. Heat 1 tbsp oil in a pressure cooker. Add jeera.
3. When it turns golden, add the dal.
4. Add salt, haldi, garam masala, red chilli powder and dhania powder.
5. Stir on low flame for 1 minute.
6. Add 1 cup water.
7. Pressure cook to give one whistle. Keep on low flame for 1 minute only. Remove from fire immediately. Keep aside.
8. To prepare the baghar, heat 3 tbsp oil in a small pan. Add sliced onions and cook till they turn brown. Remove from fire.
9. Add chilli powder. Pour the baghar over the dal. Mix gently.
10. Serve hot, garnished with shredded ginger and chopped coriander.

RICE & ROTI

ZAFRANI BIRYANI

SAFFRON FLAVOURED RICE

Serves 4

1 cup good quality basmati rice
3-4 chhoti illaichi (green cardamoms) - crushed
2 tej patta (bay leaves)
2 laung (cloves)
1 tsp butter or desi ghee
2½ tsp salt
juice of ½ lemon
8 cups water

VEGETABLE LAYER

10 - 12 french beans - cut into tiny cubes
2 carrots - cut into tiny cubes
½ cup boiled or frozen peas
2 tbsp butter or ghee
2 tbsp curd
½ tsp garam masala
½ " piece ginger - crushed to a paste or ½ tsp ginger paste
½ tsp red chilli pd
3/4 tsp salt

OTHER INGREDIENTS

4 onions - sliced and deep fried
few strands of kesar (saffron)
8-10 kaju - fried

1. Clean, wash and soak rice for 15 minutes.
2. Boil plenty of water (8 cups approx.) in a large pan. Add chhoti illaichi, tej patta, laung, salt, desi ghee or butter and lemon juice.
3. Drain soaked rice and add to the boiling water. Boil till rice is just done. See that the rice is not over cooked.
4. Strain the rice. Keep aside uncovered till it cools. Gently, separate the grains with a fork. The rice should be prepared at least 2 hours in advance.
5. Cut beans and carrots into small cubes.
6. Heat butter in a clean kadhai. Add beans and carrots. Cook, covered on low flame till vegetables are done. Add peas.

Continued...

7. Add garam masala, salt and red chilli powder.
8. Blend curd with ginger paste.
9. Add curd to the vegetables. Stir fry for 3 minutes. Keep vegetables aside.
10. Deep fry the sliced onions in a heavy bottomed kadhai, to a golden brown colour and keep aside.
11. Soak kesar in 2 tsp warm water for 10 - 15 minutes.
12. To assemble the biryani, grease an oven proof dish with butter or ghee.
13. Put half of the rice. Spread evenly with a fork.
14. Spread half of the cooked vegetables over the rice.
15. Spread a layer of fried onions using half the onions.
16. Spread the left over rice over the onions.
17. Spread the vegetables over the rice.
18. Put the left over onions on the vegetables.
19. Rub the kesar strands to extract the flavour and colour. Dot kesar on the rice at some places.
20. Garnish with fried kaju. Cover with foil and keep aside.
21. To serve, keep in a moderately hot oven for 10 minutes.

METHI TAMATAR PULAO

RICE COOKED WITH TOMATOES AND FENUGREEK

Serves 4

1 cup basmati rice - soaked for 1 hour
3 tbsp oil
½ tsp jeera (cumin seeds)
3 medium tomatoes - chopped finely
2 tbsp kasoori methi (dried fenugreek leaves)
1½ tsp salt
2 cups water (double the volume of rice)
1 tsp lemon juice

1. Soak rice for 1 hour.
2. Heat oil in a heavy bottomed pan. Reduce flame. Add jeera. Fry for about ½ minute till jeera turns golden.
3. Add chopped tomatoes and stir fry for about 5-7 minutes, mashing the tomatoes well. Continue to stir fry till oil separates.
4. Add kasoori methi and salt. Stir fry for 1 minute.
5. Add the drained rice and mix gently.
6. Add 2 cups water and lemon juice. Stir once more and cover the pan. Boil.
7. Reduce heat and simmer on low flame for about 12-15 minutes, or until the rice is cooked.
8. Allow to stand for about 3-4 minutes. Fluff with a fork to let the steam escape. Serve hot.

Aloo Matar ki Tahari

YELLOW COLOURED POTATO AND PEA RICE

Serves 4

1 cup basmati rice - soaked for 1 hour
1 medium onion - sliced finely
2 tbsp ghee or 3 tbsp oil
1 tej patta (bay leaf)
½ " piece ginger - crushed to a paste
¼ tsp haldi
1 small potato - cut into round slices
1 cup shelled peas
1½ tsp salt
2 cups water
1 tbsp chopped coriander

1. Soak rice for 1 hour.
2. Fry the sliced onion in ghee or oil until golden brown.
3. Add tej patta, ginger and haldi. Stir for 1 minute.
4. Add the potatoes and peas and stir-fry over low heat for about 2-3 minutes.
5. Add the drained rice and mix well.
6. Add salt, water and fresh coriander. Boil. Lower the flame and cook covered, for 12-15 minutes or until the rice is done.
7. Serve hot with a refreshing raita (yoghurt).

Spinach and Carrot Rice

Picture on facing page *Serves 4*

150 gm spinach (palak) - discard stems and cut leaves into thin strips (2 cups)
2 carrots - grated
1 cup basmati rice - soaked for 1 hour
2 tbsp desi ghee or oil
½ tsp saunf
2 moti illaichi (brown cardamom)
1 stick dalchini (cinnamon)
2 laung (cloves)
1 onion - sliced finely
1½ tsp salt
¼ tsp red chilli powder
2 tsp lemon juice

1. Soak rice for 1 hour.
2. Heat ghee in a heavy bottomed pan. Add saunf, moti illaichi, dalchini and laung. Stir till saunf just changes colour.
3. Add onions. Stir fry till transparent.
4. Add washed spinach and grated carrots. Stir fry for 1 minute.
5. Drain the water from the rice and add the soaked rice.
6. Add salt and red chilli powder. Add 2 cups water and lemon juice. Mix very well.
7. Boil. Lower the flame and cook covered, for 12-15 minutes or until the rice is done. Fluff it up with a fork to separate the grains.
8. Serve hot with a refreshing raita (yoghurt).

Subz Biryani

SPICY RICE WITH VEGETABLES

Serves 6-8

2 cups basmati rice - soaked for 1 hour
1-2 carrots - cut diagonally into slices
1 small cauliflower - cut into medium florets
8-10 french beans - cut into 3/4" long diagonal pieces
2 small potatoes - cut into fours
2 onions - sliced finely
½ cup oil
3 tsp salt, 1 tsp lemon juice
1 tej patta (bay leaf)

PASTE
6-7 flakes garlic
1" piece ginger
1 tbsp saunf (aniseeds)
1 tsp jeera (cumin seeds)
3 red chillies
3-4 laung (cloves)
1 tsp dhania (coriander) powder
1 stick dalchini (cinnamon)
3-4 saboot kali mirch (pepper corns)
seeds of 2 moti illaichi (brown cardamom)

1. Soak rice for 1 hour.
2. Grind the ingredients of the paste together with a little water.
3. Heat oil in a heavy bottomed pan. Add onions, cook till golden brown.
4. Add the vegetables and stir fry for 3-4 minutes.
5. Add the paste and tej patta.
6. Measure 4 cups of water and add to the vegetables.
7. Add salt and lemon juice.
8. When water boils, drain the soaked rice and add to the water.
9. Put a tawa under the pan of rice to reduce the heat further.
10. Cover the pan of rice with a small towel napkin and then with a well fitting lid. Keep some heavy weight, on the lid.
11. Slow down the fire and cook till the rice is done (10-15 minutes).
12. Serve after 10 minutes.

Miloni Tahari

MIXED VEGETABLES WITH RICE

Serves 6

1½ cups basmati rice - soaked for 1 hour
2 laung (cloves)
1 stick dalchini (cinnamon)
1 tsp garam masala
2 tsp salt
1 tsp lemon juice
5-6 tbsp oil

VEGETABLES
10 french beans - cut into 1" diagonal pieces
1 small carrot - cut into slanting slices
¼ of a small cauliflower - cut into medium florets
1 small potato - cut into four big pieces

PASTE
1 onion
2 tomato
1" ginger piece
5-6 flakes garlic

1. Soak rice for 1 hour.
2. Grind onion, tomatoes, ginger, and garlic to a paste in a mixer.
3. Cut all vegetables into big pieces. Cut beans and carrots diagonally.
4. Heat oil in a heavy bottomed pan. Add the onion-tomato paste. Cook till dry.
5. Add laung and dalchini.
6. Add the vegetables. Stir fry for 5-7 minutes, till oil separates and the masala is dry.
7. Drain the soaked rice and add to the vegetables. Mix well.
8. Add garam masala and salt. Mix.
9. Add 3 cups (double the amount of rice) water. Add lemon juice. Boil. Cover and cook on low flame till rice is done. Serve after 10 minutes.

KHUMBI GOBHI PULAO

MUSHROOM & CAULIFLOWER RICE

Serves 4

1 cup basmati rice - soaked for 1 hour
4 tbsp oil
1 medium onion - sliced
1 tsp ginger paste
1½ tsp salt
100 gm (½ packet) mushrooms - small sized
2 cups medium sized florets of cauliflower cut along with stalks
2 cups water
¼ cup fresh red, anaar ke dane (pomegranate seeds) - to garnish

1. Soak rice for 1 hour.
2. Deep fry cauliflower florets to a light golden colour.
3. Remove base of the stalks of mushrooms. Leave them whole, but if they are big, cut them into halves. Wash well. Boil 3 cups water with 1 tsp salt and 1 tsp lemon juice. Remove from fire and soak the whole mushrooms in it for 4-5 minutes. Keep aside.
4. Heat oil in a heavy bottomed pan. Add onions and fry the onions until light golden.
5. Drain the soaked mushrooms and add the whole mushrooms and stir-fry for about 4-5 minutes, till they turn brown.
6. Add ginger paste. Stir.
7. Add the fried cauliflower.
8. Drain the rice and add the rice and stir gently for ½ minute.
9. Add water and salt. Boil, lower the heat, cover and simmer for 12- 15 minutes or until the water has been absorbed and the rice is cooked.
10. Leave to stand for 5-7 minutes to allow the rice to dry out a little.
11. Serve garnished with fresh anaar ke dane or chopped coriander.

Vegetable Fried Rice

Serves 2-3

1 cup basmati rice - boiled 1 hour in advance
2 tsp salt
2 tsp lemon juice
1 tsp ginger paste
1 onion - cut into thin slices
1 cup shredded cabbage
50 gms paneer (cottage cheese) - cut into ½" cubes
1 small carrot - grated
½ cup shelled, boiled peas
green stalks of 1 spring onion - optional
½ tsp pepper powder
½ tsp red chilli powder
½ tsp garam masala
4 tbsp oil

1. Wash, soak rice for ½ hour.
2. Boil 5-6 cups of water with 2 tsp salt and lemon juice.
3. Strain the soaked rice and add to the boiling water. Stir.
4. Boil till done. Do not over cook the rice. Keep in a strainer for 5-7 minutes.
5. Transfer to a large pan. Fluff with a fork. Keep away for atleast 1 hour.
6. Boil peas in salted water with a pinch of sugar.
7. Shred cabbage into long thin strips.
8. Chop spring onion stalks into fine rings.
9. Heat 4 tbsp oil. Add onion slices. Stir fry till light brown. Add ginger paste. Cook for a minute.
10. Add cabbage and stir fry for 3-4 minutes. Do not let it turn limp.
11. Add paneer pieces and stir fry for a minute.
12. Add carrots, peas and onion stalks. Stir fry for a minute.
13. Add the rice, salt, black pepper, red chilli powder and garam masala to the rice.
14. Mix well and stir for 2-3 minutes. Add a dash of lemon juice if desired.

TOMATO RICE

Serves 4

1 cup basmati rice
4 small tomatoes - ground to a puree in a mixi
2-3 onions - chopped
¼ tsp haldi (turmeric powder)
1½ tsp salt or to taste
1 tsp red chilli powder
¼ tsp hing (asafoetida) powder

TEMPERING (CHHOWNK)
3 tbsp oil
1 tsp sarson (mustard seeds)
1 tbsp channe ki dal (Bengal gram dal)
few curry leaves

1. Clean and wash rice. Boil 5-6 cups water in a large pan. Add rice. Cook till done.
2. Strain the rice in a colander (big metal strainer). Keep aside to cool by spreading the rice in a big tray.
3. Heat oil in a karahi. Reduce flame. Add sarson and dal. Cook on very low flame till dal changes colour.
4. Add curry leaves and onions. Fry till onions turn light brown.
5. Add tomato puree.
6. Add haldi, salt and red chilli powder.
7. Cook on low flame till the dal turns soft and the tomatoes turn absolutely dry and oil separates.
8. Add hing powder.
9. Separate the rice grains with a fork and add to the tomatoes. Stir carefully till well mixed. Serve hot.

Lemon Rice

Serves 4

1 cup basmati rice

MIX TOGETHER
juice of 2 lemons
¼ tsp haldi (turmeric powder)
1 tsp sugar
1½ tsp salt or to taste

TEMPERING (CHHOWNK)
3 tbsp oil
1 tsp sarson (mustard seeds)
1 tbsp channe ki dal (Bengal gram dal)
3 dry, red chillies - broken into pieces
few curry leaves

1. Clean and wash rice. Boil 5-6 cups water with 2 tsp salt in a large pan. Add rice. Cook till done. Do not over cook.
2. Strain the rice in a colander (big metal strainer). Keep aside. Cool for ½ hour by spreading on a tray.
3. Mix lemon juice, haldi, salt and sugar together in a small bowl.
4. To temper the rice, heat oil in a big kadhai.
5. Reduce flame. Add sarson, dal and red chillies. Cook on very low flame till dal just starts changing colour. Do not let the dal turn brown.
6. Add curry leaves. Mix.
7. Add the lemon juice mixture. Add ¼ cup water.
8. Cover and simmer on low flame till dal turns soft and the water dries.
9. Separate the rice grains of the cooked rice with a fork.
10. Add rice and mix carefully till well mixed. Stir gently for 2-3 minutes. Serve hot.

Gobhi Matar Paneer Pulao

Serves 4

1 cup basmati rice - soaked for 1 hour
1 medium onion - sliced finely
2 tbsp ghee or 3 tbsp oil
1 tej patta (bay leaf)
½" piece ginger - cut into match sticks
2 laung (cloves)
1 tiny cauliflower (1 cup medium sized florets)
½ cup shelled peas
100 gm paneer (cottage cheese) - cut into ¼" cubes
2 green or 1 big red fresh chilli - slit, deseeded and cut into thin strips
1½ tsp salt
½ tsp garam masala
½ tsp red chilli powder
2 cups water

1. Soak rice for 1 hour.
2. Deep fry cauliflower florets to a light golden colour. Keep aside.
3. In the same oil, deep fry paneer cubes to a light brown colour. Soak paneer pieces in hot water after frying to make them soft. Keep aside.
4. Heat ghee or oil in a heavy bottomed pan. Fry the sliced onion until golden brown.
5. Add tej patta, ginger and laung. Stir for 1 minute.
6. Add the peas and stir-fry over low heat for about 2 minutes.
7. Add fried cauliflower and paneer pieces.
8. Add the drained rice and mix well.
9. Add salt, garam masala, red chilli powder, water and green chillies. Boil.
10. Lower the flame and cook covered, for 12-15 minutes or until the rice is done.
11. Serve hot with a refreshing raita (yoghurt).

KESARI MITHE CHAAWAL

SWEET RICE FLAVOURED WITH SAFFRON

Serves 6

2 cups basmati rice
2 cups sugar
1 small piece of fresh or dried coconut - cut into tiny pieces
4 chhoti illaichi (green cardamom) - crushed
4 laung (cloves)
2 sticks dalchini (cinnamon)
5-6 almonds - shredded
2 tpsp kishmish (raisins)
4 tbsp desi ghee
½ tsp kesar (saffron) strands - dissolved in 3 tbsp water

1. Soak rice for at least 1 hour.
2. Soak kesar in water for 10-15 minutes. Rub the threads to extract colour.
3. Cut almonds into thin long pieces and coconut into small pieces.
4. Boil 1½ cups of water with 2 cups of sugar and illaichi. Keep sugar syrup aside.
5. Heat ghee. Add laung, dalchini, coconut, almonds and kishmish. Fry for ½ a minute.
6. Add rice. Add 2½ cups of water. Boil. Cook on slow fire till water dries up and rice is almost done.
7. Sprinkle kesar along with the coloured water on the rice.
8. Strain sugar syrup into the rice. Mix gently. Continue to cook on very slow fire till rice is done and the syrup is absorbed.
9. Serve hot decorated with silver leaf.

Missi Roti

GRAM FLOUR AND WHOLE WHEAT FLOUR CHAPPATI

Serves 4

1 cup besan (gram flour)
1 cup atta (whole wheat flour)
2 tbsp desi ghee
1 tbsp kasoori methi (dry fenugreek leaves)
½ tsp salt
½ tsp red chilli pd.
½ tsp jeera (cumin seeds)
a pinch of hing (asafoetida)
¼ tsp haldi (turmeric powder)

1. Mix all ingredients. Add enough water to make a dough of rolling consistency.
2. Cover it and keep aside for ½ hour.
3. Make 6 balls.
4. Roll each ball into a chappati, but thicker than the usual chappati.
5. Cook on a hot tawa by frying it or in a hot tandoor.
6. When made in a tandoor, apply ghee and serve immediately.

BUTTER NAN

Serves 4 *Picture on page 45*

2½ cups (250 gms) maida (plain flour)
½ tsp salt
½ cup hot milk
½ tsp baking powder
½ cup warm water (approx)
a little desi ghee or salted butter
1 tsp kalaunji (onion seeds) - optional
or
1 tsp khus-khus (poppy seeds) - optional

1. Heat milk and put it in a paraat (large pan). Add baking powder to the hot milk. Mix well and keep aside for 1 minute.
2. Sift maida and salt together. Add maida to the above hot milk. Mix.
3. Knead to a soft dough with enough warm water.
4. Keep in a warm place for 3-4 hours to swell.
5. Make 6-8 balls.
6. Roll out each ball like an elongated chappati. Spread some softened butter or ghee.
7. Fold into half. Roll out to an oblong shape like the nan.
8. Sprinkle some kalaunji or khus-khus if you like. Press the seeds with a rolling pin (belan). Pull one side of the nan to give it a pointed end.
9. Apply some water on the back side of the nan. Stick in a very hot tandoor.
10. Cook till nan is ready.

Methi Wale Paranthe or Roti

Picture on page 17 *Serves 4*

2 cups atta (wheat flour)
2 cups finely chopped fresh methi (fenugreek)
1 onion - finely chopped
2 green chillies - chopped
3/4 tsp salt
½ tsp red chilli powder
¼ tsp haldi
½ tsp garam masala
2 tbsp desi ghee

1. Remove the stems of methi and chop finely. Wash well. Keep in a paraat.
2. Add wheat flour, chopped onions, green chillies, salt, red chilli powder, haldi and garam masala. Mix well.
3. Knead the flour with water. Knead to a smooth dough. Keep aside for at least 1 hour.
4. Heat the tawa (griddle). Take a ball of the dough.
5. Roll out. Spread a little ghee. Fold into half, then again into half to get a triangle.
6. Put it on the hot griddle and cook on both sides, and then fry in ghee to get a delicious parantha.

Note: For Roti take a ball of dough and roll it like a thick chappati. Cook on hot tawa by frying or in a hot tandoor. If made in tandoor, apply ghee and serve immediately.

Poodina Kulcha

Serves 6

DOUGH

250 gms maida (plain flour)
1 tsp dry yeast
¼ tsp baking powder
150 ml (3/4 cup) warm milk
1 tsp salt
1 tsp sugar
1½ tsp oil
1 tbsp curd

TOPPING

½ of a small bunch of poodina (mint) leaves - chopped
½ tsp ajwain (carom seeds) - crushed
½ tsp salt
½ tsp red chilli pd.
1 onion - very finely chopped

1. Mix 2-3 tbsp warm water with ½ tsp sugar. Add yeast. Mix well. Cover and keep aside for 10 minutes till it turns frothy.
2. Sift maida in a paraat. Add 1 tsp sugar and 1 tsp salt.
3. Put curd in the centre of the maida and sprinkle baking powder on it. Leave for a few seconds till it starts bubbling.
4. Add oil and the frothy yeast. Knead with warm milk to a dough. The dough should neither be too soft nor too stiff. It becomes loose after it is kept away for a few hours.
5. Grease a polythene, brush the dough with oil. Keep the dough in the polythene, cover it with a pan inverted over it. Keep in the sun or a warm place for 3-4 hours.
6. The dough swells. Knead it again. Keep aside.
7. Mix all the ingredients of the topping.
8. Make balls. Roll out to the desired size. Sprinkle topping all over.
9. Press gently with the rolling pin (belan) and then with your fingers.
10. Stick in a heated tandoor by applying water on the back side of the kulcha.
11. Cook till brown spots appear. Serve hot.

DAHI-RAITA
SPICED YOGHURT

Palak Raita

SPINACH IN YOGHURT

Serves 4-5

20 leaves of palak - very finely chopped and washed
½ tsp salt, ¼ tsp red chilli powder
2½ cups curd (yoghurt)
seeds of 1 moti illaichi (black cardamom) - crushed to a powder
¼ tsp roasted jeera (cumin) powder

1. Boil 3 cups water in pan. Place the leaves in a metal strainer with big holes (colander) and place the colander on the pan of boiling water. Cover the colander and steam the palak for 3 minutes. Remove from fire and cool the leaves. Alternately, boil the leaves by dropping them in boiling water for 3 minutes. Strain and cool.
2. Beat curds till smooth.
3. Add palak, salt, moti illaichi powder and red chilli powder to the beaten curd. Transfer to a serving dish. Sprinkle with bhuna jeera and red chilli powder.

Poodina Raita

YOGHURT WITH MINT

Serves 4-5

½ kg curd - 2½ cups
1 cup poodina (mint) leaves - ground to a paste
1 tsp powdered sugar
¼ tsp kala namak (rock salt)
salt and red chilli powder to taste

1. Beat curd well, preferably with an electric beater.
2. Wash poodina leaves well and grind to a paste.
3. Add a little poodina paste to the beaten curd, just enough to get a light green colour. Mix well. Keep the rest of the mint paste in the refrigerator for future use.
4. Add powdered sugar, salt, chilli powder and kala namak to taste. Keep in the fridge till serving time.

BHARWAAN DAHI-BHALLE

FRITTERS IN YOGHURT

Makes 12 pieces

BHALLAS (FRITTERS)

1 cup urad dhuli dal (split black beans)

½" piece ginger

1 green chilli

2 pinches of hing (asafoetida)

FILLING (MIX TOGETHER)

1 tsp finely chopped ginger

1 tsp finely chopped almonds

1 tsp finely chopped green chillies

12-15 pieces kishmish - soaked in water for 10 minutes

a pinch of salt

DAHI (YOGHURT)

½ kg curd (2½ cups)

salt to taste

½ tsp kala namak

1 tsp powdered sugar

1 tsp roasted jeera (cumin seeds) powder

½ tsp red chilli powder

CHUTNEY

1 tbsp amchoor (dry mango powder)

3 tbsp sugar or gur

½ tsp bhuna jeera (roasted cumin powder)

½ tsp red chilli powder

salt to taste

1. Clean, wash dal. Soak in water for about 4 hours.
2. Strain. Grind with minimum amount of water along with the other ingredients given under bhallas to a thick batter.
3. Beat the batter preferably with an electric beater or with your fingers, adding a few drops of water occasionally.
4. After beating, the mixture should look frothy and a ball of this mixture should float when dropped in water.

Continued .....

5. Heat oil to medium hot temperature.
6. Wet your palms with a little water. Put a ball of the batter on your left palm, put in some filling and flatten the ball. Transfer it gently on your wet, right hand fingers and slowly slip into the hot oil with the help of the thumb.
7. Deep fry 5-6 pieces at a time.
8. Heat 6 cups of water with 2 tsp salt. Drop 4 - 5 fried bhallas. Leave in water for ½ minute. Turn them. Remove from water after a few seconds.
9. Squeeze them gently. Keep in the fridge.
10. Beat curd very well, preferably with an electric egg beater.
11. Add all the other ingredients. Chill the prepared curd.
12. Mix all ingredients of the chutney together in a small heavy bottomed pan and cook on low flame till thick. Remove from fire.
13. Dip the prepared bhalle in dahi and arrange in a dish. Sprinkle some chutney. Garnish with chopped coriander leaves with a sprinkling of red chilli powder and roasted jeera powder.
14. Serve with extra chutney and dahi.

Mixed Fruit Raita

Serves 4-5

½ kg curd - 2½ cups
½ small apple - peeled and cut into tiny pieces
8-10 black or green grapes - halved
1 small boiled potato - cut into tiny pieces
1 tbsp chopped coriander
½ tsp powdered sugar
salt to taste
¼ tsp kala namak (rock salt)
½ tsp red chilli pd.
3/4 tsp roasted jeera (cumin seeds) powder

1. Beat curd till very smooth.
2. Add sugar, salt, kala namak, chilli powder and roasted jeera powder. Mix well.
3. Add small pieces of apple, potato and grapes. Mix in some chopped coriander.
4. Transfer to a serving dish. Sprinkle a few grape halves, a little red chilli powder and jeera powder.

Raita Anaarkali

Serves 4-5

½ kg curd - 2½ cups
1 cup red anaar ke dane (fresh pomegranate seeds) (1 anaar)
1 tbsp besan ki boondi
1 tsp roasted jeera (cumin seeds) powder
½ tsp chilli pd.
salt to taste - ½ tsp approx.

1. Beat curd till smooth.
2. Mix all ingredients.
3. Keep in the fridge till serving time.

South Indian Raita

TEMPERED RAITA

Serves 4-5

½ kg curd - 2½ cups
½ cup grated coconut (remove the brown skin before grating)
1 cup finely shredded cabbage
¼" piece ginger - grated finely
2 green chillies- chopped finely
salt to taste

BAGHAR
1 tbsp oil
½ tsp sarson (mustard seeds)
½ tsp jeera (cumin seeds)

1. Beat curd.
2. Mix cabbage, coconut, ginger, green chillies and salt.
3. Heat 1 tbsp oil in a small pan. Reduce flame and add jeera and mustard seeds.
4. When they crackle, pour over the prepared raita. Keep in the fridge.

Cabbage & Carrot Raita

Serves 4-5

½ kg curd (2½ cups)
½ cup finely grated carrot
½ cup finely grated cabbage
1 tbsp finely chopped coriander
salt to taste
1 tsp powdered sugar
1 tsp roasted cumin (bhuna jeera) powder

1. Beat curd.
2. Mix all other ingredients. Transfer to a serving dish. Sprinkle some bhuna jeera and red chilli powder.
3. Keep in the fridge till serving time.

SAVOURY SNACKS

Kale Channe ke Kababs

FLATTENED BALLS OF BLACK GRAM

Serves 12

BOIL TOGETHER

½ cup kale channe (black gram)
1 tbsp channe ki dal (split gram)
¼ tsp jeera (cumin seeds)
1" stick dalchini (cinnamon)
seeds of 1 moti illaichi (brown cardamom)
3-4 laung (cloves)
3-4 saboot kali mirch (pepper corns)
2 flakes garlic - optional
½" piece ginger
1 dry, red whole chillies
1 onion - chopped
2 slices bread - dipped in water and squeezed
¼ tsp amchoor (dry mango powder)
salt to taste

1. Soak channas and channe ki dal together in about 2½ cups water, for 6-8 hours or overnight.
2. Pressure cook channas with jeera, dalchini, moti illaichi, laung, kali mirch, garlic, ginger and red chilli to give one whistle. Keep on low heat for 20 minutes.
3. If there is any water left, dry the channas on fire, leaving just a little water enough to grind.
4. Grind to a fine paste. Add bread, salt and amchoor to taste.
5. Chill the mixture in the fridge for sometime.
6. Make small flattened rounds.
7. Deep fry 4-5 pieces in medium hot oil. Drain on absorbent paper.
8. Sprinkle onion rings over the kababs. Garnish with chopped poodina leaves.

Note: If the kababs break on frying, add another slice of crumpled bread to the mixture. The kababs may also be rolled in maida and then fried.

UPMA

SEMOLINA WITH PEAS

Serves 6

1½ cups suji (semolina)
1 tsp sarson (mustard seeds)
1 tsp jeera (cumin seeds)
2-3 dried red chillies
1½ tbsp channe ki dal (split gram)
1 tbsp urad dhuli dal (split black beans)
2 onions - chopped finely
3½ cups water
½ cup shelled, boiled or frozen peas
juice of 1 large lemon
1½ tsp salt
10-12 curry leaves - optional
½ cup oil

1. Roast suji in a karahi on low flame, stirring continuously, for about 5 minutes. Do not let it change colour.
2. In a clean heavy bottomed karahi, heat oil. Add jeera and sarson together.
3. When these splutter, switch off the fire. Add the red chillies and dals.
4. Stir till dals turn light brown. Return to fire.
5. Add onions. Fry till brown.
6. Add water. Add peas, salt and lemon juice. Boil water.
7. Cover and cook on low flame for 5-7 minutes till the dal is cooked and is no longer crunchy.
8. Add suji gradually with one hand and stirring with the other hand continuously, keeping the flame low.
9. After all the suji has been added, stir fry the upma for 2-3 minutes.
10. Add 2 more tsp oil and fry some more. Serve hot.

Cottage Cheese Squares

SMALL AND DAINTY SQUARES!

Serves 6

1/3 cup suji (semolina)
1 cup milk
1 cup (150 gms) paneer (cottage cheese) - grated
¼ cup coriander leaves - chopped
salt to taste
¼ tsp garam masala
½ tsp red chilli powder
1½ tsp lemon juice
bread crumbs
oil for frying

BATTER FOR COATING

1 tbsp maida (plain flour) dissolved in about ¼ cup water to make a thin batter

1. Roast suji in a karahi on slow fire for 2-3 minutes. Do not let it turn pink.
2. Add milk, stirring continuously. Cook till thick. Keep on low flame for 1-2 minutes more, stirring constantly, until dry and forms a lump.
3. Remove from fire. Add paneer, lots of fresh coriander, salt, chilli powder, garam masala and lemon juice. Mix very well. Keep the salt and spices, a little on the higher side.
4. Grease a flat plate or a tray. Make a big ball of the paneer mix and roll on the greased plate, such as to oil it. Set this mixture in the form of a big square 4" x 4" and ¼" thick on the plate. Let it set for at least 15-20 minutes.
5. Cut into 1" neat squares.
6. Heat oil. Dip squares in the coating batter.
7. Roll in bread crumbs and deep fry 2-3 pieces at a time.

Note: If home made paneer is used, it should be squeezed well to drain of all the liquid (whey).

KHANDAVI

GRAM FLOUR ROLLS TEMPERED WITH MUSTARD SEEDS

Makes 8 rolls

½ cup gram flour (besan)
3/4 cup curd
3/4 cup water
½ tsp salt, ¼ tsp haldi
pinch of hing (asafoetida)
½" piece ginger - crushed to a paste
1 green chilli - crushed to a paste

TEMPERING (BAGHAR)
1½ tbsp oil
½ tsp rai (mustard seeds) - crushed
1 green chilli - chopped fine (optional)
few coriander leaves - chopped
a little freshly grated coconut

1. Mix besan, curd and water well with a beater so that no lumps remain.
2. Add haldi, salt, ginger, chilli paste and hing.
3. Cook the mixture till it is of quite thick consistency, stirring continuously, till the mixture turns thick.
4. Remove from fire.
5. Spread quickly, thinly on a plastic sheet. Let it cool for 5-7 minutes. Cut into thin strips (1" broad) & make rolls.
6. For the baghar, heat oil.
7. Add rai & green chilli. Let it crackle.
8. Add coriander leaves and coconut. Mix and pour over the prepared khandavi.

Aloo Chaat

SHALLOW FRIED SPICY POTATOES

Serves 4

4-5 boiled potatoes of medium size
1½ cups shelled, boiled peas
1" piece of ginger - chopped finely
2-3 green chillies - chopped finely
1 tbsp chaat masala (store the excess)
½ lemon
5-6 tbsp oil
salt to taste

CHAAT MASALA

¼ cup roasted saboot dhania (coriander seeds)
¼ cup amchoor (dried mango pd.)
¼ cup red chilli powder
¼ cup roasted jeera (cumin seeds)
¼ cup salt
¼ tbsp (kala namak) rock salt
½ tbsp saboot kali mirch

1. Prepare the chaat masala by grinding dhania, jeera, kali mirch and kala namak together.
2. Mix amchoor, red chilli powder and salt. Store in an air tight container.
3. Cut boiled potatoes into one inch pieces.
4. Shallow fry the potato pieces on a tawa or frying pan till brown on all sides.
5. Remove the fried potatoes from the pan. Keep aside.
6. In 1 tbsp of oil fry ginger for ½ minute in the frying pan on low flame.
7. Add peas and stir fry for 1 minute, keeping the flame low. Remove from fire.
8. Mix potatoes, green chillies, lemon juice and salt. Add chaat masala to taste.
9. Garnish with fresh coriander leaves.

Methi-Pyaz Pakoras

DRIED FENUGREEK & ONION FRITTERS

Makes 12-14 pieces

1 cup besan (gram flour)
2 tsp oil
3/4 tsp red chilli powder
¼ tsp haldi powder
½ tsp garam masala
¼ tsp ajwain (carom seeds)
salt to taste - 3/4 tsp approx.
1 tsp lemon juice
¼ tsp baking powder
2 small onions - sliced finely
4 tbsp kasoori methi (dry fenugreek leaves)

1. Mix besan, oil, red chilli powder, haldi, garam masala, ajwain, lemon juice and salt with enough water to make a thick batter like heavy cream. Beat well till the mixture is smooth.
2. Add baking powder. Beat well to make the batter light.
3. Add kasoori methi and onions. Mix well.
4. Drop spoon fulls in hot oil. Deep fry pakoras to a light golden colour. Keep aside.
5. At the time of serving, press the fried pakoras slightly and fry once again in hot oil till brown and crisp.

Pao Bhaji

MIXED VEGETABLES STIR FRIED ON A GRIDDLE & SERVED WITH BUNS

Serves 6

200 gms (3) boiled potatoes - mashed roughly
½ cup shelled peas
200 gms (½ flower) cauliflower - chopped finely
250 gms (1 small flower) cabbage - chopped finely
1 carrot - chopped
6-8 french beans - chopped finely (optional)
250 gms (4) tomatoes - chopped finely
250 gms (3 big) onions - chopped finely
1" piece ginger
4-6 flakes garlic - optional
2 dry red chillies
2 tbsp Pao-Bhaji masala
50 gms butter, 4-5 tbsp oil
1½ tsp salt or to taste
1 tbsp chopped coriander

1. Chop all vegetables finely. Mash potatoes roughly.
2. Pressure cook peas, cauliflower, cabbage, carrots and beans with ½ cup water to give one whistle.
3. Grind ginger, garlic and chillies to a paste.
4. Heat oil. Add onions and cook till transparent.
5. Add ginger paste and cook for 2-3 minutes.
6. Add pao-bhaji masala and salt.
7. Add tomatoes and cook for 5-7 minutes. Mash them well, while they are being cooked. Sprinkle 2-3 tbsp water occasionally.
8. Add pressure cooked vegetables. Cook for a few minutes. Mash well while cooking.
9. Add potatoes. Stir fry till well blended.
10. Add butter and chopped coriander. Keep bhaji aside.
11. Slice 2 small onions finely. Sprinkle some salt, red chilli powder and lemon juice to taste.
12. To serve, cut buns (pao) into halves. Heat a tawa or a non-stick pan. Put 1 tbsp butter on it. Press the paos in butter, heating till they turn soft. Serve with hot bhaji, dotted with butter. Serve onions mixed in lemon juice along with pao-bhaji.

Gobhi Samosa

TRIANGULAR PATTIES STUFFED WITH CAULIFLOWER

Serves 6-8

DOUGH

1 cup maida (plain flour)
1/3 tsp salt
3 tbsp ghee (vanaspati) or margarine

FILLING

1 medium cauliflower - grated
2 small boiled potatoes - mashed coarsely
¼" piece ginger - grated
½ tsp red chilli pd., salt to taste
3/4 tsp roasted jeera pd. (cumin seeds)
3/4 tsp garam masala
¼ tsp amchoor (dried mango pd.)
1 tbsp broken cashewnuts
1 tbsp kishmish (raisins)
2 green chillies - finely chopped
¼ tsp sugar

1. Mix all ingredients of the dough.
2. Add a few tbsp of water and knead to form a semi hard dough.
3. Keep dough covered for ½ hour.
4. To prepare the filling, heat 3 tbsp oil. Put off the fire. Add ginger. Add salt, red chilli powder, garam masala, jeera, and amchoor.
5. Return to fire. Add nuts. Cook for a few seconds.
6. Add potatoes. Cook for ½ minute.
7. Add cauliflower. Mix well. Add sugar and green chillies.
8. Cover and cook on slow fire till the cauliflower is cooked. Make the filling spicy. Keep aside.
9. Make big lemon sized balls of the dough. Roll out thinly. Cut into two.
10. Fold each half into a triangle to form a cone.
11. Seal the cone by applying water. Fill 1 tbsp of the filling in the cone.
12. Make a small fold or pleat on the side, opposite to the joint.
13. Now close the cone with water. Press the side opposite to the pointed side against a plate, giving it a samosa look.
14. Heat oil. Deep fry 8-10 pieces at a time on low heat.

Bharvaan Aloo Tikki

SAVOURY POTATO CAKES

Serves 6

4 boiled potatoes - medium size
2 slices of bread
1 tsp red chilli pd.
½ tsp garam masala (mixed spices)
salt to taste
½ tsp chaat masala

FILLING

1/3 cup urad dhuli dal (split black beans)
½ tsp haldi (turmeric pd.)
1 tbsp oil
½" ginger - chopped finely
1 green chilli - chopped finely
1 tbsp chopped coriander
½ tsp garam masala and red chilli pd.
salt to taste
a pinch of hing (asafoetida)
½ tsp chaat masala

1. Boil 3 cups of water with ½ tsp salt and ½ tsp haldi. Add cleaned and washed dal. Boil on low flame for about 20 minutes, till dal gets cooked. Strain the dal. Keep boiled dal aside.
2. Mash potatoes. Remove crust of bread slices and dip in water. Immediately remove from water. Squeeze well to remove water.
3. Mix potatoes, bread, red chilli pd, garam masala, chaat masala and salt.
4. Heat 1 tbsp oil. Add hing. Add ginger, chopped coriander and green chillies. Add boiled dal. Add chaat masala, garam masala, salt and red chilli powder. Cook for 2-3 minutes on low flame.
5. Make balls of big size with the potato mixture. Flatten each ball. Make a slight depression in the centre. Put 1 tbsp of dal filling in the centre.
6. Form a ball again. Flatten to form a tikki.
7. Heat 1/3 cup oil in a non-stick pan or a tawa. The oil should not be too much. Fry only 2-3 pieces at one time. Shallow fry till brown and crisp.
8. Remove from oil on paper. Slit the tikki horizontally. Serve with chutney.

Masala Suji Idli

SEMOLINA PATTIES

Picture on facing page

Makes 8 pieces

1 tbsp oil
1-2 green chillies - chopped finely
1 cup suji (rawa) - coarse semolina
2 tbsp chopped coriander leaves
½ tsp soda-bicarb
1 cup curd
¼ cup finely grated coconut - optional
½ cup water
3/4 tsp salt

GARNISH

1 small tomato - cut into slices, a few curry leaves

1. Chop coriander leaves and green chillies finely.
2. Heat 1 tbsp oil in a kadhai.
3. Add chillies. Stir fry for ½ minute.
4. Add coarse suji (rawa). Mix well. Stir fry for 2-3 minutes, on medium flame, stirring continuously. Remove from fire.
5. Add coriander leaves and salt. Mix well. Allow to cool.
6. Add coconut, curd, water and soda-bicarb. Beat well. Keep aside for 10 minutes.
7. Grease small katoris or the idli stand. Arrange a tomato slice and a curry patta in each katori or mould.
8. Pour 2-3 tbsp mixture in it.
9. To steam, put 1" water in a big pressure cooker or a big pan with a well fitting lid and keep it on fire.
10. Place the idli mould inside the cooker and put the lid after removing the whistle. Keep the gas on full flame.
11. After the water boils and the steam starts coming out, reduce flame. Keep for 15 minutes on medium flame. Insert a clean knife to see if the idli is done. If it sticks to the knife, steam for another 3-4 minutes.
12. Switch off the fire and remove the idlis from the mould with a clean knife, after cooling for 5 minutes.
13. Serve hot with coconut chutney and sambhar given on page 67.

SPINACH ROLLS

Serves 10

DOUGH

1 cup maida (plain flour)
½ of a small potato - boiled and grated
½ tsp salt
2 tsp oil
milk - to knead

FILLING

4 cups chopped palak (spinach)
1 onion - chopped finely
a pinch of mitha soda (soda-bicarb)
2 green chillies - chopped
4 tbsp mashed paneer (cottage cheese)
2 tbsp oil
½ tsp each of salt, red chilli powder and garam masala

SEALING PASTE

2 tbsp maida dissolved in 3 tbsp water
2 tsp amchoor (dried mango pd.)
2 onions - finely chopped

1. Sift maida and salt together. Add finely grated potato.
2. Add 2 tsp oil. Knead with a little milk to a soft dough. Keep aside.
3. Make 10 small, marble sized, balls. Roll out into very thin chappatis.
4. Cook like a chappati, on both sides, on a tawa (griddle). Keep aside.
5. To prepare filling, heat oil. Add onions, cook till onions turn transparent.
6. Add chopped palak, green chillies and mitha soda. Cook for 5-7 minutes on low flame, till palak gets cooked. Add salt, red chilli powder, garam masala and paneer. Mix well. Remove from fire.
7. Mix amchoor in 4 tsp water. Spread some amchoor paste on each chappati. Sprinkle some chopped onion over it.
8. Spread palak mixture over it. Roll the chappati.
9. Join the edges with the sealing paste.
10. Heat 1-2 tbsp oil on a tawa and cook the rolled chappati in oil on low flame, till light brown.
11. Cut into rolls and serve hot.

SWEETS

Phirni

BLANCMANGE

Picture on page 1

Serves 6

3½ cups (700 gm) milk
1/3 cup sugar (slightly less than ½ cup) or to taste
4 almonds (badam) - shredded
5-6 green pista (pistachio) - shredded
2 small silver leaves-optional
¼ cup basmati rice or rice flour
2-3 chhoti illaichi (green cardamom) - powdered
1 drop kewra essence
or
1 tsp ruh kewra

1. Soak rice of good quality for about an hour and then grind very fine with 4 to 5 tablespoonfuls of cold water (rice flour may be used as a substitute). Dissolve the rice paste in some more milk and make it thin.
2. Mix the rice paste with the milk in a heavy bottomed pan. Cook on medium heat, stirring continuously, till the mixture is of creamy consistency.
3. Add sugar and cardamom powder and stir.
4. Simmer till it is fully dissolved and then boil 1 minute.
5. Remove from fire and add ruh kewra or the essence and half of the shredded almonds and pistachios.
6. Pour the mixture into 6 small glass bowls.
7. Chill. Decorate each dish with a silver leaf and a few shredded nuts.

Date and Walnut Rolls

Makes 10 pieces

250 gms dates - deseeded and chopped
1 cup milk
1½ tbsp malai or desi ghee
½ cup walnuts - broken into bits
1 tbsp dessicated coconut

1. Wash, clean dates. Remove seeds and chop them.
2. Pressure cook chopped dates with 1 cup milk.
3. After the first whistle, keep on low heat for 15 minutes. Remove from fire.
4. When the pressure comes down, mash the dates.
5. Add ghee or malai and cook till the dates stop sticking to the bottom of the cooker.
6. Remove from the cooker and mix in the walnuts nicely.
7. Shape into a roll. Roll over dessicated coconut. Keep in the fridge in a container.
8. At the time of serving, cut into slices.

SUJI KA HALWA

SEMOLINA PUDDING

Serves 4

1 cup suji (semolina)
6 semi heaped tbsp of desi ghee or vanaspati
1 cup sugar
2 cups milk
2 cups water
4 chhoti illaichi (green cardamom) - skinned and crushed
1/8 tsp orange colour
8-10 kishmish (raisins)
1 tbsp pista - cut into thin long pieces
8-10 almonds - cut into thin long pieces
1 sliver leaf

1. Mix milk, water, kishmish, crushed illaichi, orange colour and sugar.
2. Boil. Remove from fire.
3. Stir to dissolve the sugar. Keep aside.
4. Heat ghee in a karahi. Fry suji on low heat till it just changes its colour.
5. Add milk mixture, stirring continuously for 7-8 minutes till the halwa leaves the sides of the karahi.
6. Remove from fire.
7. Keep in a serving dish. Decorate with sliver leaf, shredded almonds and pista.
8. Serve hot.

MEETHI SUKHI SEVIYAN

SWEET VERMICELLI

Serves 4

1 cup Bambino vermicelli or thick home made vermicelli
½ cup sugar
2 tbsp desi ghee
8 -10 almonds - cut into thin long pieces
1 tbsp kishmish (raisins)
2-3 chhoti illaichi (green cardamom) - skinned and crushed
2 cups water
50 gms khoya (dried whole milk) - optional

1. Boil sugar, water and crushed chhoti illaichi. Remove from fire. Keep the sugar syrup aside.
2. Fry vermicelli in ghee on slow fire in a karahi till brown.
3. Add kishmish and shredded almonds. Cook for a few seconds. Switch off the fire.
4. Add the sugar syrup. Boil. Keep covered on slow fire till the syrup is dry and the vermicelli is cooked.
5. Serve hot garnished with crumbled khoya and whole almonds.

Rice Kheer

RICE PUDDING

Serves 4-5

1 cup boiled rice
1 kg (5 cups) full cream milk
1/3 cup sugar
2 tbsp milk powder
3-4 chhoti illaichi (green cardamom) - crushed
10-12 almonds - shredded
8-10 pista (pistachio) - shredded
1 tbsp kishmish (raisins)
1 drop kewra essence
1 silver leaf

1. Dissolve milk powder in a little milk. Keep aside.
2. Boil the rest of the milk in a heavy bottomed kadhai or pan, with cooked (boiled) rice. Reduce flame.
3. Add sugar, dissolved milk powder and illaichi. Cook on low flame till thick.
4. Keep mashing occasionally to break the rice grains.
5. When it reaches the right consistency, (thick pouring) add nuts and kishmish, keeping aside a few for the top.
6. Add just 1 drop of essence.
7. Pour into a serving dish. Decorate with silver leaf. Spread whole almonds and shredded pista.
8. Serve hot kheer during the winter and rainy months and chilled kheer during the hot summer days.

PISTA KULFI - I

INDIAN ICE CREAM

Picture on page 1 *Serves 15*

1 kg (5 cups) full cream milk - at room temperature
1 tin (400 gms) milkmaid (condensed milk)
2 tbsp cornflour
3-4 chhoti illaichi (green cardamom) - crushed
1 tbsp shredded pista (pistachio), 1 tbsp shredded almonds

1. Open the tin of milkmaid in a heavy bottomed pan.
2. Dissolve cornflour in ¼ cup milk.
3. Add the rest of the milk gradually to the milkmaid, stirring continuously.
4. Mix well. Add illaichi. Keep on fire. Boil.
5. Add the cornflour paste to the boiling milk, stirring continuously.
6. Continue boiling, by lowering the flame, for about 5 minutes. Cool.
7. Add pista and almonds.
8. Fill in clean kulfi moulds and leave to set in the freezer for 6-8 hours or overnight.

PISTA KULFI -II

Picture on page 1 *Serves 8*

1 kg - (5 cups) full cream milk
½ cup sugar
2 tbsp cornflour
75 gms fresh khoya - grated and mashed slightly
1 tbsp pista (pistachio) - very finely cut
1 tbsp almonds - very finely cut
3-4 crushed chhoti illaichi (green cardamom)

1. Dissolve cornflour in 1 cup milk and keep aside.
2. Boil the rest of the milk in a karahi till it is reduced to half in quantity, for about 20 minutes on medium fire.
3. Add sugar and cornflour paste. Cook for 2-3 minutes more till the sugar is well dissolved.
4. Remove from fire. Cool slightly.
5. Add khoya, almonds, pista and crushed illaichi.
6. Fill the mixture in the kulfi moulds. Freeze for 6-8 hours or overnight.

Shahi Tukri

INDIAN BREAD PUDDING

Picture on facing page

Serves 6

4 slices bread
2½ cups milk
1/3 cup sugar
5-6 chhoti illaichi (green cardamom) - skinned and crushed
a few strands of kesar (saffron) dissolved in 1 tbsp water
75 gms khoya (dried whole milk)
4-5 almonds - cut into thin long pieces
4-5 pista (pistachio) - cut into thin long pieces
1 sliver leaf
4 tbsp desi ghee

1. Remove the side crusts of bread. Cut each slice into 3 pieces.
2. Fry in 4-5 tbsp ghee till golden brown. Keep aside.
3. Heat milk to which sugar and illaichi have been added. Boil. Remove from fire.
4. Dip 4-5 fried slices in the hot milk. Keep them soaked for a few seconds.
5. Remove slices from milk and arrange in a flat serving plate.
6. Repeat with the other slices.
7. Mash khoya and add to the left over milk.
8. Cook this milk till it thickens and turns into rabri (15-20 minutes).
9. Pour the hot rabri over the toasts.
10. Decorate with silver leaf.
11. Sprinkle shredded almonds and pista. Dot with soaked kesar.
12. Serve warm or cold, according to the weather.

Gajar ka Halwa

CARROT PUDDING

Picture on page 1

Serves 4

½ kg carrot - grated into long shreds
1 cup milk
¼ cup sugar
2-3 tbsp desi ghee
5-6 badam (almonds) - shredded
10-12 kishmish
3-4 chhoti illaichi (green cardamom) - powdered
100 gms khoya - grated

1. Boil milk in a clean karahi.
2. Add grated carrots and cook uncovered, stirring occasionally, till milk dries.
3. Add badam and kishmish. Stir for 1 minute.
4. Add sugar. Cook till the mixture turns dry again.
5. Add ghee and stir fry for 10 minutes on low flame.
6. Add grated khoya. Mix well. Serve hot.

Kesari Mishti Dahi

SAFFRON FLAVOURED FRUITY CURD

Serves 4-6

3 cups milk
1 tsp cornflour dissolved in ¼ cup milk
6-7 tsp sugar
2½ tsp fresh curd - for starter (jaag)
1 tsp kesar (saffron) - dissolved in 1 tbsp hot milk
8-10 grapes - cut into tiny pieces
or
segments of ½ orange - pieces peeled

1. Boil milk and sugar in a pan. Reduce flame.
2. Add cornflour paste, stirring continuously.
3. Rub the kesar strands to extract flavour. Add to the milk.
4. Keep milk boiling on medium flame to thicken, for 10 minutes, stirring frequently.
5. Remove milk from fire. Cool till luke warm.
6. Put 2½ tsp curd in a serving dish. Mix with a spoon. Add thickened milk which should be luke warm.
7. Pour the milk back into the empty pan.
8. Add tiny bits of fruit to the milk (optional) and then pour it back into the serving dish. Keep undisturbed in a warm place for 3-4 hours till set.
9. Chill in the fridge for 3-4 hours before serving. Serve chilled.

PICKLES & CHUTNEYS

NIMBOO KA ACHAR

LIME PICKLE

250 gm fresh limes
65 gm salt
260 ml mustard oil (sarson ka tel)
A grain of asafoetida (hing) of the size of a peppercorn
1 heaped teaspoonful of chilli powder (lal mirch)
125 gm ginger (adrak) - sliced
8 gm brown mustard seeds (sarson)
15 gm whole red chillies
15 gm green chillies (sabz mirch) - sliced
7 gm ground fenugreek seeds (methi dana)
Juice of 6 limes
45 gm salt

1. Wash and dry the limes with a clean dry cloth.
2. Make 4 cuts in each lime, rub the salt all over and insert into the cuts.
3. Keep in a jar for about 2 to 3 weeks and shake every alternate day.
4. After about 3 weeks, heat the oil till blue haze appears.
5. Remove from the fire, add asafoetida (hing) and crush with the back of a spoon when it swells up.
6. Add chilli powder and heat till the red colour comes out but it is not burnt.
7. Take the pan off the fire, add brown mustard seeds (sarson) and stir till it is cooked.
8. Add ginger (adrak), green chillies and the limes cut into 4 pieces.
9. Simmer till the ginger and the limes are a little tender.
10. In the meantime roast the fenugreek seeds on a hot griddle (tawa) and then grind.
11. Also take out the juice of six limes.
12. Add both these to the cooked pickle, stir and simmer for 2 to 3 minutes.
13. Remove from the fire, cool and pour into a sterilised screw-capped glass jar.
14. Cover and tie a piece of muslin around the neck of the bottle.

Navrattan Chutney

SPICY MANGO CHUTNEY

450 gm grated raw green mangoes - peeled and grated
120 ml water
4 bay leaves (tej patta)
5 teaspoonfuls salt
60 gm dried dates (chuawara)
100 ml vinegar
455 gm sugar
1 teaspoonful red pepper (degi mirch)
1 teaspoonful black cumin seeds (kala jeera)
1 teaspoonful ground cinnamon (dalchini)
½ teaspoonful ground cloves (laung)
½ teaspoonful ground nutmeg or mace (jaiphal or javetri)
¼ teaspoonful crushed peppercorns
1 teaspoonful ground ginger (sonth)
¼ teaspoonful crushed brown cardamom (moti illaichi)
60 gm toasted almonds (badam) - sliced
60 gm raisins (seeds removed) (munacca)
30 gm pistachio nuts (pista)
1 tablespoonful fresh lime (nimboo) juice

1. Wipe the dry dates and pressure cook them in vinegar till soft. Remove the dates from the vinegar, cool and slice thinly. Keep remaining vinegar aside.
2. Put the grated mango in a heavy bottomed stainless steel pan. Add water, tej patta and salt.
3. Cover and simmer on slow fire till it becomes a little soft. Stir every now and then to prevent sticking of the shreds to the bottom of the pan. Remove from fire when cooked.
4. Make a syrup with sugar and the remaining vinegar of the dates.
5. Add cooked mango-shreds, thinly-sliced dried dates, red pepper and black cumin seeds, cinnamon, cloves, nutmeg, cardamoms and black pepper corns. Cook till it becomes a thick puree.
6. Add the sliced toasted almonds, raisins, pistachios and lime juice. Simmer gently until thick.
7. Remove from heat. Cool, and pour into sterilised jars.

Aloo Bukhara Chutney

DRIED PLUM CHUTNEY

230 gm dried plums (alu bukhara)
4 teaspoonfuls salt
30 gm almonds
30 gm sultanas (kishmish)
1 teaspoonful powdered dried ginger (sonth)
1 teaspoonful roasted ground white cumin seeds (sufaid zeera)
½ teaspoonful garam masala
125 gm gur (molasses)
30 gm pistachio nuts (pista)
4 teaspoonfuls vinegar
¼ teaspoonful black salt (kala namak)
A few drops of tomato colouring
750 ml water

1. Soak the dried plums and the dates overnight in 750 ml water.
2. Boil them in the same water for 15 minutes.
3. Take off the fire, cool and separate the dates.
4. Remove the stones from the plums, mash and pass the pulp through a fine sieve.
5. Add gur (molasses) and colouring and cook till it is of creamy consistency.
6. In the meantime blanch the nuts and the sultans; peel the skins of the nuts and shred them fine.
7. Remove the stones from the boiled dates and chop them fine.
8. Mix the shredded nuts, sultanas, cumin seeds, garam masala, ginger, vinegar, black salt and the chopped dates into the plum puree.
9. Bring to the boil, add colouring, cool and pour into sterilised bottles. This chutney, like the coriander and mint chutney, should be used within 1 or 2 days of its preparation. It can be stored in a refrigerator for 4 days.

Gajar ka Murabba

CARROT PRESERVE

Serves 4

455 gm carrots (gajar)
½ teaspoonful citric acid (nimboo ka sat)
455 gm sugar
4 drops kewra essence
or
1 teaspoonful ruh kewra

1. Select medium-sized carrots.
2. Scrape off the skin, cut into halves and prick all over.
3. Mix sugar and the carrots in a stainless steel pan and leave them overnight.
4. Next day, add citric acid and cook on low flame till the carrots become soft and the syrup thickens to one-thread consistency.
5. Remove them from the heat. Cool.
6. Add kewra essence or ruh kewra.
7. Pour into a hot clean dry glass jar.

Am ka Murabba

GREEN MANGO PRESERVE

1 kg raw green mangoes
720 ml water
60 gm toasted blanched almonds
1 teaspoonful citric acid (nimboo ka sat)
6 drops kewra essence
or
1 tablespoonful ruh kewra
1½ kg sugar
8 green cardamoms (seeds only)

1. Wash, peel, cut the mangoes into large slices and prick all over with a fork.
2. Tie the slices loosely in a piece of muslin, and simmer for 5 to 7 minutes in 720 ml of boiling water.
3. Remove and dry them on a piece of cloth.
4. Add sugar and citric acid to the water in which mango slices were boiled.
5. Cook to one-thread consistency. Remove the scum from the surface of the syrup.
6. Add mango slices, simmer till the syrup thickens and the slices become tender and slightly translucent.
7. Leave for 12 hours.
8. Remove the slices from the syrup if they are sufficiently tender.
9. Tie the crushed cardamom seeds in a piece of muslin and add this to the syrup.
10. Boil till it again acquires one-thread consistency.
11. Remove the muslin containing the cardamom seeds, squeeze out the juice and discard the seeds.
12. Add mango slices and peeled halves of blanched almonds and cook for a few minutes more.
13. Remove from the heat and cool. Add ruh kewra or essence and put into hot clean glass jars.